Cheiro's Book of Numerology

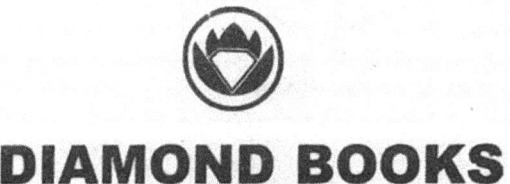

© **Publisher**

Publisher	:	**Diamond Pocket Books (P) Ltd.**
		X-30, Okhla Industrial Area, Phase-II
		New Delhi-110020
Phone	:	011-40712200
E-mail	:	wecare@diamondbooks.in
Website	:	www.diamondbooks.in
Edition	:	2025
Printed by	:	Repro (India)

Publisher's Note

'Numbers' form a significant aspect of our life. Nobody can imagine a day of life without them. And so they affect the ways that we are, act, feel and relate to others. Each of us has our own special mixture of numbers, everyone of which represents our potential qualities. The study of numbers as the figures designating the year of one's birth, to determine their influence on one's life is what is popularly known as 'Numerology.' Hence Numerology is a kind of tool which helps one to meditate and know oneself and others.

It has been established by scientific observation that there are only Nine Planets in our Earth's Solar System that relate to life in this world. It has also been demonstrated by scientists that an exactly similar Solar System is repeated in the molecules revolving round all atoms in nature.

In the same way there are only Nine Numbers by which all calculations on this earth are made. Beyond the numbers 1 to 9, the rest are repetitions, a 10 being simply a 1 with a zero, an 11 is 1 plus 1, a 2; a 12 is 1 plus 2, a 3; and so on. Every number no matter how large, can be reduced to a single figure by what is called "natural addition" adding from left to right. The final single digit that remains is called the "spirit or soul number" of the previous numbers added together.

It therefore follows that all Birth dates come into the 1-9 scale and respond to the numbers given to the Nine Planets of our Solar System. A person born on the 10th, 19th or 28th of a month is as equally a "Number One" individual, as the one born on the 1st of a month. Their characteristics vary according to the position of their month in the Zodiac.

Cheiro's book on Numerology has precisely looked into all such aspects like the significance of birth number and name number; what they represents; their effect; as well as the remedies to offset the influence of unlucky numbers. The uniqueness of the book lies in the fact that even a layman will be able to understand the various aspects being discussed and make calculations accordingly.

CONTENTS

1. The Significance of Numbers 7
2. The Planetary Numbers of the Months 18
3. The Effect of 'Single' Numbers on men and women 22
4. The Significance of Number 1 23
5. The Significance of Number 2 26
6. The Significance of Number 3 29
7. The Significance of Number 4 32
8. The Significance of Number 5 35
9. The Significance of Number 6 38
10. The Significance of Number 7 41
11. The Significance of Number 8 44
12. The Significance of Number 9 49
13. The Occult Symbolism of 'Compound' Numbers 53
14. The 'Compound' or 'Spiritual' Numbers 61
15. How to Use 'Single' and 'Compound' Numbers 69
16. Why the Birth Number is the Most Important 72
17. Some Illustrations of Names and Numbers 76
18. How Numbers Recur in Lives 79
19. The Unfounded Dread of the Number '13' 81
20. The Similarity of Numbers in the Lives of St. Louis and Louis XVI 83
21. Periodicity in Numbers 86
22. The Philosphy of Numbers 91
23. How to Find the 'Lucky' Day 96
24. Colours and Numbers 98
25. The Value of Concentration in Regard to One's Number 100
26. Combinations Between 1-4 Persons and Uniqueness of the Numbers 4 and 8 102
27. More About Persons Born Under the Numbers 4 and 8 104
28. The Affinity of Colours and Numbers and How Music and Numbers are Associated 107
29. Numbers and Disease : Planetary Significance of Herbal Cures 110
30. How to Know What City, Town or Place is Fortunate for One to Live in 115
31. Horse-racing and Numbers 120
32. Names and Numbers of Some of the USA Heads 122
33. The Bible and Numbers 129
34. Conclusion 136

1. THE SIGNIFICANCE OF NUMBERS

The ancient Hindu explorers of Nature's laws, it must be remembered, were in former years masters of all such studies, but in transmitting their knowledge to their descendants, they so endeavoured to hide their secrets from the common people that in most cases the key to the problem became lost, and the truth that had been discovered became buried in the dust of superstition and charlatanism, to be re-formed, let us hope, when some similar cycle of thought in its own appointed time will again claim attention to this side of nature.

This ancient people, together with the Chaldeans and Egyptians, were the absolute masters of the occult or hidden meaning of numbers, in their application to time and in their relation to human life.

When examining such questions, we must not forget that it was the Hindus who discovered what is known as the precession of the Equinoxes, and in their calculation such an occurrence takes place every 25,827 years; our modern science after hundreds of years of labour has simply proved them to be correct.

How, or by what means they were able to arrive at such a calculation, has never been discovered—observations lasting over such a period of time are hardly admissible, and calculation without instruments is also scarcely conceivable, and so science has only been able, first to accept their statement, and later to acknowledge its accuracy.

Their judgement, together with that of the Chaldeans, as to the length of what is now known as the cycle of years of the planets, has been handed down to us from the most remote ages, and also by our modern appliances, which has been proved correct. While studying the value of numbers 1 to 9, it is necessary to assume that as the seven harmonies of music form the basis of all music that has ever been conceived, these numbers form the basis of all our numbers and calculations. Then only we can logically accept the decisions of those great students of long past ages and at least examine their deductions with a mind free from bias and prejudice.

It is impossible here to give in detail all the reasonings and examples that exist for a belief in the occult side of numbers, but it may interest my readers if I give a few illustrations of why the number 7 has for ages been regarded *as the number of mystery relating to the spiritual side of things* and why the number 9 has in its turn come to be regarded as *the finality or end of the series on which all our materialistic calculations are built,* but the most casual observer can only admit that beyond the number 9 all ordinary numbers become but a mere repetition of the first 9 numbers. A simple illustration of this will readily suffice. The number 10, as the zero is not a number, becomes a repetition of the number 1. The number 11 added together as the ancient occultists laid down in their law of *natural addition,* namely adding together from left to right, repeats the number 2, 12; repeats 3, 13; repeats 4, and so on up to 19, which in its turn becomes 1 plus 9 equals 10, and so again the repetition of 1. 20 represents 2, and so on to infinity. The occult symbolism of what are called compound numbers, that is, those numbers from 10 onwards, shall be dealt with later.

In this way it will be seen that we are compelled to build all our *materialistic* systems of numbers, on the numbers 1 to 9 taking them as the base, just as we take the seven great or primary harmonies in music as the basis of all music, and again as the seven primary colours are the basis of all our combinations of colours. In passing, it may be remarked that all through the Bible and other sacred books, the 'seven', whenever mentioned, always stands in relation to the spiritual or *mysterious force of the Almighty,* and has a curious significance in this sense whenever employed.

A few instances can be taken to prove this point. Genesis (in the Bible) refers to seven days (or cycles) of the creation. We quite often comes across a reference to the seven heavens, the seven thrones, the seven seals and the seven churches. The reference to the seven days' march round the walls of Jericho, when, on 'the seventh day,' the walls fell, *before that mysterious God-force* is symbolised in the number of seven. It is also remarkable that there are exactly seven generations from David to the birth of Christ. In *Revelation* we read of the 'seven spirits of God sent forth into all the earth.' *Ezekiel* speaks of 'The seven angels of the Lord that go to and fro through the whole earth,' which is believed to be a reference to the magnetic influences of the seven creative planets which radiate through the earth. Again, we have the seven Spirits referred to in the Egyptian religion, the seven Devas of the Hindus, the seven Amschaspands of the Persian faith, the seven Angels of the Chaldeans, the seven Sephiroth of the Hebrew Cabala, the seven Archangels of Revelation, etc.

Let us now take another view of this strange number. If we were to examine every class of occult teaching from the Hindus, Chinese, Egyptian, Greek, Hebrew or modern school, whichever one may choose, in every case, without a single exception, we shall find that the quality of the number 7 stands for the aforementioned expression of that mysterious God force in Nature.

In the most ancient rules of occult philosophy we find the rule laid down that the number 7 is the only number *capable of dividing 'the number of Eternity,'* and continuing in itself as long as the number representing Eternity lasts, and yet, *at every addition of itself producing the number 9* or in other words it produces the basic numbers on which all materialistic calculations are built and on which all human beings depend and the whole edifice of human thought finds expression.

Example : The number 1 represents the First Cause, Creator, God or Spirit, call it as you like. A circle or the zero, '0,' has always been taken as the symbol of endlessness or eternity. Place the 1 and the figure zero by its side, and you get the significant symbol of eternity such as 1 plus 0, the 10, and then, place as many of these emblems of eternity by its side as you like, and you get such a figure as 1,000,000. Divide this figure by the mystic number 7 and you get the number 142857.

$$7 \overline{)1,000,000}$$
$$142857$$

Add as many zeros as you like, and keep on dividing by the 7, and you yourself may go on through all eternity and you can only get repetitions of the same 142857, which from time immemorial has been called the 'sacred number.' Now add this number by natural addition and it will give you the figure 27, and as you have seen by the rule of natural addition described on a preceding page, you keep adding till only one number remains, to arrive at what is known as 'the root of the number.' You again add 27 by natural addition, and 2 plus 7 equals 9 or in other words, you get the full range of the first series of numbers on which all *materialistic or human calculations can be built.*

Now, let us return to the symbolism of seven for a moment. You know, of course, that Buddha is always represented as sitting in the centre of a Lotus. Let us examine, then the secret of such a selection. It is not perhaps generally known that the 7 is reproduced in many strange ways by Nature herself, and that flowers that have not been crossed by intermingling with other flowers have their outside petals in the number of seven. But as flowers are so easily crossed with other varieties, and it is so difficult to find a pure type, Buddha took the Lotus, which can never be crossed and which never loses its individuality, as the emblem of the religion he taught, because, first of all, its seven foundation petals are always in evidence, and further, the religion he taught maintained that the creative Spirit was the foundation and origin of all things, and thus bore a silent but unmistakable testimony to the creative action of the seven planets from which all religions have had their origin.

Long before man made his creeds or civilisations their laws, the influence of these seven planets had become known on the earth. Out of the dark night of antiquity their light became law and as far as we can penetrate, even to the very confines of prehistoric days, in all races, in all countries, we find the influence of the seven planets through all and in all.

Days of the Week

The seven days of the week have been the outcome of the influence of the seven creative planets and the days of the week came to be named after them in every land or clime. Take any nation, you may find that, this fact remains the same, and is so expressed in almost every language—Chinese, Assyrian, Hindi, Egyptian, Hebrew, Greek, Latin, French, German or English. Monday or Moonsday in English becomes Montag in German and Lundi (Lune) in French, Lunes in Spanish, and so on until one comes to Saturday or Saturn's day, the day on which God ordered the Hebrews that no work should be done, and while giving them this command He said, 'It is a sign between Me and the children of Israel forever.'[1] And Saturday, year by year, in our modern civilisation is becoming more and more a day of rest.

---

[1] Wherever the Jews went they obeyed this command, even causing their Roman conquerors and other pagan nations to follow their example. Josephus wrote: 'There is not a city of the Grecians, nor any of the barbarians, nor any nation, whither our custom of resting on the seventh day hath not come.' The seventh day of the Jews is Saturday, called the Sabbath derived from the Hebrew word Sabbath which means to rest.

In connection with this thought, it is worthy to remark that Saturn, the last planet in the series of the seven creative planets of our solar system, in all religions, Hebrew or otherwise represents 'cessation,' or rest from labour in another sense. In this strange example one can see the connection between the seven days of the week and the seven creative planets, and it throws a new light on the verse, 'God made the sun, moon, and stars and appointed them for signs and *for seasons and for days and for years.'* Even Mr. Maunder, the eminent author of so many works on astronomy, calls attention to this strange division of the week into seven days when he says in his *Astronomy of the Bible:* 'the period of seven days does not fit precisely into either months or seasons of the year. It is not a division of time *that man would naturally adopt, it runs across all natural division of time.'* But this author, not seeing or perhaps not knowing the great hidden truth contained in the number 7, worried only over the point, that it was not a division of time *which man would naturally adopt.* But as everything on the earth and above the earth has its meaning, and has its secret or soul —its place, position, and number, in the 'order of things,' which is the highest form of design, *every day of the week, every hour of the day, and every minute of the hour, has both its meaning and number.*

It is invariably conceded by every class of scientist that the regularity, order, and system of the wonderful machinery of the heavens is beyond comparison.

We know today that the heavenly bodies move through their orbits with such precision that in millions of years they do not vary one minute of time. We know that they exercise an influence on this earth which is felt by the veriest atoms in the earth, though what this force is or with what incredible speed it acts, may forever remain a mystery. It was in dealing with this mysterious law that the ancient philosophers by study, experiments, concentration of mind, and perhaps intuition, arrived at the fixation of certain laws governing life, which may be as accurate as their discovery that the 'precession of the Equinoxes takes place once in every 25,827 years.'

It is from these wonderful students of Nature that we have received the first idea as to the divisions of the Zodiac into twelve periods of 30 degrees, and further, that each period produces a definite and well-known influence on the earth and on human beings born in any of its twelve periods. They further subdivided these 30-degree periods into division of three periods of 10 degrees each, in which the planets are also found to have an influence, and they pursued their investigations until they worked out a system demonstrating that each day had its own particular meaning due to vibrations in the ether, which keeps the earth in instantaneous rapport with its entire solar system, and lastly, that as the sun enters a new degree of the Zodiac in mid-winter at about the rate of every 2½ to 3 minutes, and in summer at the rate of 3 to 4¾ minutes, that its magnetic influence varied the effect of the vibrations or ether waves of each planet, and so enabled these students of Nature to carry their system in this way down to almost the smallest fraction of time.[1]

In examining this subject, let us take for an example any remarkable piece of mechanism we may have seen, such as a clock. We have noticed how wheel fits into wheel and how the entire mechanism is put into motion as the ray or tooth of the governing wheel presses against the tooth of the next, and so on.

Keeping this illustration in your mind for a moment, let us regard the 360 degrees of the Zodiac into which the sun appears to pass, from degree to degree on an average of every 4 minutes as the teeth of one of our wheels. This 360 degrees multiplied by the 4 minutes gives 1,440 minutes, and this, divided by 60, to bring it to hours, gives us the 24-hour day, which becomes in its turn another spoke in the great wheel of time, and consequently, by the advance of the sun, must bring us to the commencement of another day under new and distinct influences, and so on until the year itself is completed.

Now as science proves that it takes the sun 30 days to pass from one division of the Zodiac into another, again we have the illustration of another wheel, as it were, but a still slower one, being put into motion, and consequently with the change in the heavenly mechanism another set of influences are brought to bear upon the earth, and so on until the twelve months of the year have in their turn experienced the influence of the sun in the twelve divisions of the Zodiac.

Let us now return for a moment to the part played by the seven creative planets. No one today, I believe, can plead ignorance of the effect of one of these planets, namely the moon, on the earth and also on the people who inhabit the earth. We all know or at least have heard

---

[1] This applies, of course, to the motion of the the sun through the symbolic or cabbalistic Zodiac used in the East.

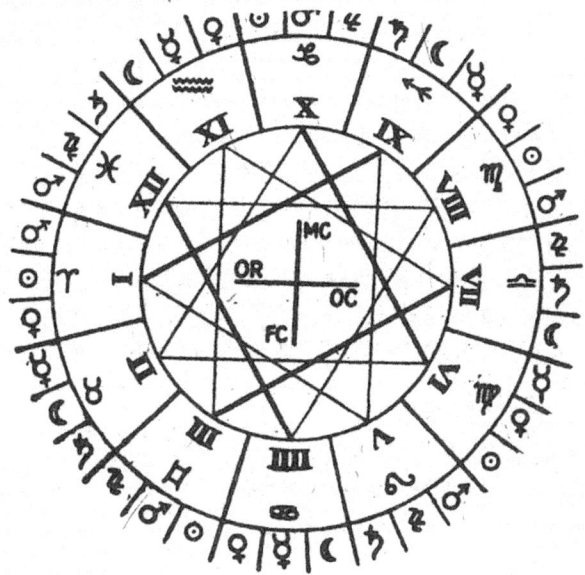

FIGURE 1

Map showing the Twelve Divisions of the Zodiac, each division sub-divided into three parts of 10 degrees.

SIGNS OF THE ZODIAC   **SIGNS OF THE SEVEN PLANETS**

I. Aries, the Ram — The Sun
II. Taurus, the Bull — Venus
III. Gemini, the Twins — Mercury
IV. Cancer, the Crab — Moon
V. Leo, the Lion — Saturn
VI. Virgo, the Virgin — Jupiter
VII. Libra, the Balance — Mars
VIII. Scorpio, the Scorpion
IX. Sagittarius, the Archer
X. Capricorn, the Goat
XI. Aquarius, the Water-Bearer
XII. Pisces, the Fishes

This map represent the Sun's entry into Aries in the Vernal Equinox on March 21-23 of every year. The letters at the points of the central cross stand for : OR—Oriental or Eastern; MC—Mid-Heaven; OC—Occidental or Western; FC—Lower Heaven.

of, about the effect of the moon on the brain of people mentally unbalanced. We know how it causes tides to rise and fall along our shores, but still perhaps we do not realise that even in the deepest ocean its pull or attraction is so great that it causes hundreds or thousands of tons of dead weight of water to be drawn up to such a height as 70 feet in the Bay of Fundy and in the Bristol Channel.

Scientists, like Darwin in England, Flammarion in France, and others in Germany, made the startling discovery that there are actually tides *in the solid earth itself,* which are affected by the attraction of the moon. What then of the effect of the moon on the brain itself, which contains the most subtle essence and is one of the greatest mysteries known in life ? If this can be considered true, what about the part played on human nature by the rest of the planets, which are in each individual case far larger than the moon?

The following table showing the dimensions of each of the planets will more explicitly illustrate my argument.

Diameter of	Mercury	2,000	miles
	the moon	2,100	miles
	Venus	7,510	miles
	the Earth	7,913	miles
	Mars	4,920	miles
	Jupiter	88,390	miles
	Saturn	71,900	miles
	Uranus	33,000	miles
	Neptune	36,000	miles
	the Sun	860,000	miles

After glancing through this above given illustration, is it logical to admit the effect of the moon and to deny effect of the other planets that are infact much larger than it?

Let us now return to the important side of the question as regards the rules set forth in this book. You will very naturally ask, how and when were such numbers arrived at that represent the mechanical action or influence of the celestial system on the people of this earth ? I could write an entire volume on this side of the question alone, but in the following necessarily condensed pages you will find the general law explained which may be sufficient to elucidate the system contained in the following chapters.

In the first place, the secret or occult significance of numbers was revealed to man so far back in the world's history that the exact place of their discovery has never been recorded, but it suffices to state that if one goes back in one's investigations to the most distant period in the history of any race who made themselves in any degree responsible for such studies, even there one would find that these numbers representing the qualities of the solar system and the basis of all our later forms of calculation existed.

In working out the idea contained in these pages, I have carefully investigated every important form of occultism bearing on this question, but whether it has been Hindu, Egyptian, Chaldean or Greek, the symbols of these numbers have always appeared the same, and their relation to months, days, hours, and people representing certain numbers, has been more or less alike.

The description of the 'secondary numbers' in the subsequent pages, even though brought into a practical form by myself, is the result of a long investigation and experience extending over many years. Although we may never be able to find out the exact time in past ages when the influence of these numbers was discovered, that is no reason why we should not accept what has been given to us by those ancient students. There are many other things we are forced to accept in life just being conscious of their truth, even when we are not able to get back to their birth or beginnings.

The origin of life we know not, but we are none the less conscious that life exists. The balance, poise, and hidden laws governing our own solar system have also never been explained, together with a thousand other things in our everyday life. The very origin of numbers is itself a mystery; yet we are forced to employ them, and as Balzac says, 'without them, the whole edifice of our civilisation would fall to pieces.'

In the *Book of the Wisdom* of Solomon, now included in the Apocrypha, Solomon says:

> For God Himself gave me an unerring knowledge of the things that are, to know the constitution of the world, the beginning and the end and middle of times, the alterations of the solstices, the changes of seasons and the positions of the planets the nature of living creatures and the thoughts of men, all things that are either secret or manifest I learned, for He that is the artificer of all things taught me this wisdom.

I ask, could anything be more forcible or convincing than such a statement, particularly when it is remembered that the true Seal of Solomon was none other than the seven-pointed star which contained the nine numbers which constitute the base of all our calculation, and which is the root of the system of numbers as applied to human life?

Even in our chemistry we have given a number and symbol to all the elements.

Water is 1010 and its symbol is H_2O
Hydrogen is 212 and its symbol is H
Oxygen is 1030 and its symbol is O
Nitrogen is 1969 and its symbol is N
Carbon is 1050 and its symbol is C

All occult studies point to the fact that the ancient students had a foundation for ascribing to every human being *his number in the universe,* and if we admit, as we do that there is a moment for birth and a moment for death, so also in the links of years, days, and hours, that make up the chain of life, it is not illogical to assume that *every link of life has also both its number and place.* I claim that by such a study man may become more perfect by his fitting in with the laws, system, and order of things to which he owes his being .

There is evidence that those ancient students were conversant with the fact that there were two distant planets than Saturn in our solar system, for they assigned beyond 'the seven creative planets' the orbits for two more heavenly bodies and they described them as governing the thoughts *on the mental side of Nature* and not the physical, and their description of them is in exact accordance with our present-day knowledge of the effect of the recently discovered planets of Uranus and Neptune on human life.

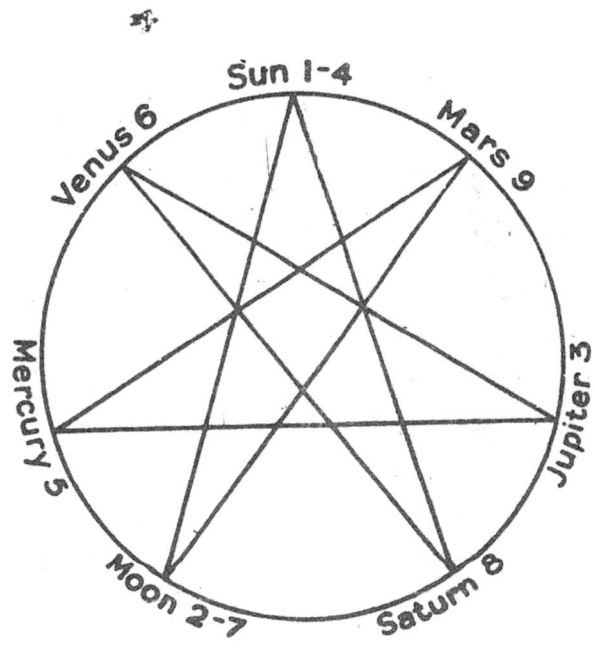

FIGURE 2 : The Seven-pointed seal of Solomon

The Sun, with the numbers 1-4, represents the combination of the Sun and the planet Uranus (the male quality of Creation being the Sun with the feminine Uranus *of the mental or spiritual plane)*. The Moon, with the numbers 2-7, represents the Moon and Neptune, the Moon being feminine on the material or earth plane while Neptune being masculine *on the mental or spiritual plane.*

The meaning of the lines of the Star : That Life starts from the Sun–proceeds to the Moon, from that to Mars, from Mars to Mercury, from Mercury to Jupiter, from Jupiter to Venus, from Venus to Saturn, and from Saturn (symbol of death) it returns to the Sun–or God from whence it came–to begin all over again in another cycle, and *so on through eternity.*

2. THE PLANETARY NUMBERS OF THE MONTHS

Although later in these pages the reader will find how the single and compound numbers have their particular meaning in connection with human life, it is better to understand at this stage how and why the months have received their particular numbers.

The true solar year commences with the Sun's entrance into the Vernal or Spring Equinox on the 21st to the 23rd day of March of every year, and appears to pass through each Sign of the Zodiac of 30 degrees each, one after the other, taking slightly under 365 ¼ days to do so, making our year popularly accepted as comprising of 365 days.

The Earth, completing its one rotation on its own axis in 24 hours, causes the whole of the 13 signs of the Zodiac in their turn to pass over each portion of the Earth once each 24 hours. The Moon revolves round the earth in a lunar month of 28 days. This wonderful mechanism, if I may call it so, is exactly like the hour-hand, minute-hand, and second-hand of a clock.

What is called the first sign of the Zodiac is the 'period of the number 9' or the Zodiacal Sign of ARIES, from 21st March to 19th April. It is ruled by the planet Mars in its *positive* aspect, and has '9' as its number.

The 'period of the number 6' is the Zodiacal Sign of TAURUS from 21st April to 20th May. It is ruled by the planet Venus in its *positive* aspect, and has '6' as its number.

The 'period of the number 5' is the Zodiacal Sign of GEMINI, from 21st May to 20th June. It is ruled by the planet Mercury in its *positive* aspect, and has '5' as its number.

The 'period of the 2 and 7' is the Zodiacal Sign of CANCER, from 21st June to 20th July. It is ruled by the Moon in its *positive* aspect, and has the double figure of '2-7' as its number.

The 'period of the 1 and 4' is the Zodiacal Sign of LEO, from 21st July to 20th August. It is ruled by the Sun in its *positive* aspect, and has the double figure of '1-4' as its number.

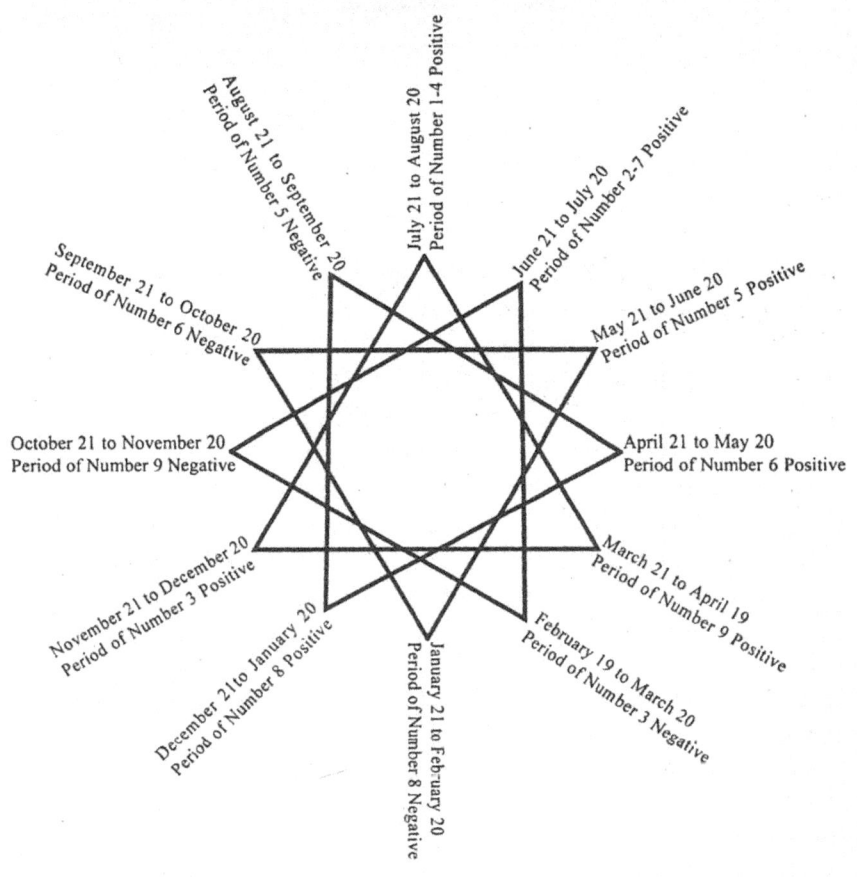

FIGURE 3 : The four divisions of the zodiac - Fire, Water, Air, Earth

THE FIRE TRIANGLE
1st "House," March 21 to April 19.
2nd "House," July 21 to August 20.
3rd "House," Nov. 21 to Dec. 20.

THE AIR TRIANGLE
1st "House," May 21 to June 20.
2nd "House," Sept. 21 to Oct. 20.
3rd "House," Jan. 21 to Feb. 19.

THE WATER TRIANGLE
1st "House," June 21 to July 20.
2nd "House," Oct. 21 to Nov. 20.
3rd "House," Feb. 19 to March 20.

THE EARTH TRIANGLE
1st "House," April 21 to May 20.
2nd "House," August 21 to Sept. 20.
3rd "House," Dec. 21 to Jan. 20.

The 2nd 'period of the number 5' is the Zodiacal Sign of VIRGO from 21st August to 20th September. It is ruled by the planet Mercury in its *negative* aspect, and has '5' as its number.

The 2nd 'period of the number 6' is the Zodiacal Sign of LIBRA from the 21st September to the 20th October. It is ruled by the planet Venus in its *negative* aspect, and has '6' as its number.

The 2nd 'period of the number 9' is the Zodiacal Sign of SCORPIO, from 21st October to 20th November. It is ruled by the planet Mars in its *negative* aspect, and has '9' as its number.

The 'period of the number 3' is the Zodiacal Sign of SAGITTARIUS, from 21st November to 20th December. It is ruled by the planet Mars in its positive aspect, and has '3' as its number.

The 'period of the number 8' is the Zodiacal Sign of CAPRICORN, from 21st December to 20th January. It is ruled by the planet Saturn in its *positive* aspect, and has '8' as its number.

The 2nd 'period of the number 8' is the Zodiacal Sign of AQUARIUS, from 21st January to 20th February. It is ruled by the planet Saturn in its *negative* aspect, and has '8' as its number.

The 2nd 'period of the number 3' is the Zodiacal Sign of PISCES, from 19th February to 20th March. It is ruled by the planet Jupiter in its *negative* aspect, and has '3' as its number.

This brings us back to the point from which we started. Owing to the Sun passing from one Sign of the Zodiac to another, seven days are allowed at the begining of each sign and seven days at the end, which is called the 'Cusp of the Sign'. During this period the number of the month and the qualities it represents *are not quite so strong* as during the rest of the period and partakes to a certain extent *of the qualities of the Sign which is passing away* with those of the one *that is coming into action*. It will be observed that the planets have a Positive and Negative quality in accordance with the period of the Zodiac they rule; the Positive giving the more physical and forceful qualities, the Negative the mental. For example, the symbol of the *9 positive,* the Sign of Aries is a man in armour with his visor closed and a naked sword in his hand.

The *9 negative* in the Sign of Scorpio is also represented by a man in armour, but with the visor up showing his face, and the sword in its sheath, symbolic of the mental warrior rather than the physical.

The Sun and the Moon are the only two planets having what is called 'double numbers,' because the Sun and Uranus are interrelated to one another, so the number of the Sun is written as 1-4. The Moon being interrelated with Neptune is written as 2-7.

A curious thing, and one well worth noting, is that there appears to be a sympathy and attraction between the numbers 1-4 and 2-7, and it will be found that persons born under any of the 1-4 numbers, such as the 1st, 4th, 10th, 13th, 19th, 22nd, 28th, and 31st, are sympathetic and get on well with people born under the numbers 2-7, such as the 2nd, 7th, 11th, 16th, 20th, 25th, and 29th and more especially so if either of these two sets of people is born in the 'House of the Moon,' namely between June 20th and July 21st-27th or in the 'House of the Sun,' between July 21st and August 20th-27th.[1]

The Number given to the Days of the Week are as follows:

Sunday	1-4	Thursday	3
Monday	2-7	Friday	6
Tuesday	9	Saturday	8
Wednesday	5		

These numbers correspond to the Planets as follows:

Sun	1	Venus	6
Moon	2	Neptune	7
Jupiter	3	Saturn	8
Uranus	4	Mars	9
Mercury	5		

---

[1]NOTE : — I have added the seven days of the 'Cusp' to each of these periods.

3. THE EFFECT OF SINGLE NUMBERS (1 TO 9) ON MEN AND WOMEN

There is no getting away from the fact that there are only nine planets in our Solar System, also that there are only nine numbers by which all our calculations on this earth are made. Beyond these nine numbers all the rest are repetitions, as 10 is a 1 with a zero added, an 11 is 1 plus 1, a 2; a 12 is 1 plus 2, a 3; and so on; every number, no matter how high, can be reduced to a single figure by what is called 'natural addition' from left to right. The final single number that remains is called the 'spirit or soul number' of all the previous numbers added together.

In the first part of this study there are only nine numbers to be considered, and one has but to master the occult meaning of each of these nine numbers as they occur in the Birth dates of men and women to find a key to the secrets of human nature that will be of great interest.

I will endeavour to write as simply as possible that all who read may clearly understand what these numbers mean, even in the most ordinary day to day actions of life. Without going into any elaborate description of why this or that influence has been given to any particular number, I will without more preamble go straight to the subject, and show how each person may find what their number may be and how they may utilise this information.

The nine numbers we have got to study are: 1, 2, 3, 4, 5, 6, 7, 8, and 9. These numbers were given to the planets that control our system in the most distant ages of civilisation, and have been used and adopted by all students of occultism, Chaldean, Hindu, Egyptian or Hebrew.

The secret underlying the whole idea is that of the mysterious law of vibration. The day of Birth giving a key number that is related to the planet bearing the same number, represents a vibration that lasts all through life, and which may or may not be in accordance with the 'Name number,' which I will explain later, and with the vibration of individuals with whom we are brought into contact.

First we must consider each number in relation to the planet it represents.

4. THE SIGNIFICANCE OF NUMBER 1

The number 1 stand in this symbolism for the Sun. It is the beginning—that by which all the rest of the nine numbers were created. The basis of all numbers is one—the basis of all life is one. This number represents all that is creative, individual, and positive. Without going into further details, a person born under the Birth number of 1 or any of its series, has the underlying principles of being in his or her works creative, inventive, strongly individual, definite in his or her views, and in consequence more or less obstinate and determined in everything they undertake individually. This relates to all men and women born under the number 1, such as on the 1st, 10th, 19th or 28th of any month (the addition of all these numbers making a 1), but more especially so if they happen to be born between 21st July and 28th August, which is the period of the Zodiac called the 'House of the Sun,' or from the 21st March to 28th April, when the Sun enters the Vernal Equinox and is considered elevated or all-powerful. It is for this reason, which you will observe has a logical basis, that people born under the number 1 in these particular periods must bear certain character traits more distinct to them.

People born under '1' are ambitious; dislike restraint, always rise in their respective profession or occupation. They have an inborn desire to head the organisation they work in and as departmental chiefs they maintain their authority and exudes respect from their subordinates.

These people should endeavour to carry out their most important plans and ideas on all days that vibrate to their own number, such as on the 1st, 10th, 19th or 28th of any month, but especially in periods from 21st July to 28th August, and from 21st March to 28th April. These people get on well with persons born under the numbers—2, 4, and 7, such as those born on the 2nd, 4th, 7th, 11th, 13th, 16th, 20th, 22nd, 25th, 29th, and 31st, especially those born in the strong periods indicated.

The days of the week most fortunate for number 1 persons are Sunday and Monday, and especially so if one of their 'own numbers' should also fall on that day, such as the 1st, 10th, 19th or 28th, and next to that their interchageable numbers of 2, 4, 7, such as the 2nd, 4th, 7th, 11th, 13th, 16th, 20th, 22nd, 25th, 29th or 31st.

The most fortunate colours for persons born under the number 1 are all shades of gold, yellows and bronze to golden brown. Their 'lucky' jewels are the topaz, amber, yellow diamond, and all stones of these colours. If possible, they should wear a piece of amber.

FAMOUS PEOPLE BORN UNDER THE NUMBER 1

Alexandar the Great	1st July	Represents a	1
James I	28th June	"	1
Charles I	19th Nov.	"	1
George I	28th May	"	1
George II	10th Oct.	"	1
Duke of Wellington	1st May	"	1
General Gordon	28th Jan.	"	1
President Garfield	19th Nov.	"	1
'General' Booth	10th April	"	1
Field-Marshal Earl Haig	19th June	"	1
Queen Alexandra	1st Dec.	"	1
Field-Marshal Lord French	28th Sept.	"	1
David Livingstone	19th Mar.	"	1
Lord Charles Beresford	10th Feb.	"	1
Annie Besant	1st Oct.	"	1
President Wilson	28th Dec.	"	1
President Monroe	28th April	"	1
President Hoover	10th Aug.	"	1
Orville Wright	19th Aug.	"	1
Sven Hedin	19th Feb.	"	1
Chopin	1st March	"	1
William Dean Howells	1st March	"	1
Bismarck	1st April	"	1
Sir Edwin Arnold	10th June	"	1
Sir Robert Ball	1st July	"	1
John Calvin	10th July	"	1
Mary Anderson	28th July	"	1
Alexandre Dumas	28th July	"	1

Oliver Wendell Holmes	28th Aug.	Represents a	1
President Adams	19th Oct.	"	1
'Cheiro'	1st Nov.	"	1
Delcasse	1st Nov.	"	1
William Hogarth	10th Nov.	"	1
Captain Cook	28th Oct.	"	1
Danton	28th Oct.	"	1
Goethe	28th Aug.	"	1
Oliver Goldsmith	10th Nov.	"	1
Ferdinand de Lesseps	19th Nov.	"	1
Thomas More	28th May	"	1
Nensen	10th Oct.	"	1
Sir Charles Napier	10th Aug.	"	1
Charles Stewart Parnell	28th June	"	1
Adelina Patti	10th Feb.	"	1
Edgar Allan Poe	19th Jan.	"	1
Lord Russell of Killowen	10th Nov.	"	1
Sir H.M. Stanley	28th Jan.	"	1
Brigham Young	1st June	"	1
Brigitte Bardot	28th Sept.	"	1
Twiggy	19th Sept.	"	1
Richard Burton	19th Nov.	"	1
Charles Laughton	1st July	"	1

5. THE SIGNIFICANCE OF NUMBER 2

Symbolically number 2 stands for the Moon. It has the feminine attributes of the Sun, and, for this reason alone, although number 1 and number 2 people are decidedly opposite in their characters, their vibrations are harmonious and they make good combination.

Number 2 persons are gentle by nature, imaginative, artistic and romantic. Like the number 1 people, they are also inventive, but they are not as forceful in carrying out their ideas. Their qualities are more on the mental than the physical plane and they are seldom as strong physically as those born under the number 1.

Number 2 people are all those who are born on 2nd, 11th, 20th or 29th in any month, but they have more marked characteristics if they are born between 20th June and 27th July, this period being what is called the 'House of the Moon.' I have added the seven days of the 'Cusp' to 20th July.

Number 2 and number 1 people vibrate together, and in a lesser degree with number 7 people, such as those born on the 7th, 16th or 25th in any month. Number 2 persons should endeavour to carry out their chief plans and ideas on days whose numbers vibrate with their own, such as on the 2nd, 11th, 20th or 29th of any month, but more especially during the period of 20th June to 27th July.

The days of the week more fortunate or 'lucky' for them are Sunday, Monday and Friday (the reason Friday is favourable in this case is that it is governed by Venus), and especially so, if, like the number 1 people, one of their own numbers should fall on either of these days, such as the 2nd, 11th, 20th or 29th, and next to these their interchangeable numbers of 1, 4, 7, such as the 1st, 4th, 7th, 10th, 13th, 16th, 19th, 22nd, 25th, 28th or 31st.

The chief faults they should guard against are—becoming restless and unsettled, lack of continuity in their plans and ideas, and lack of self-confidence. They are also inclined to be oversensitive, and too easily get despondent and melancholy if they are not in happy surroundings.

People born under the number 2 should wear all shades of green, from the darkest to the lightest, also cream and white, for these are their 'lucky colours. But as far as possible they should avoid all dark colours, especially black, purple and dark red.

Their 'lucky' stones and jewels are pearls moonstone, pale green stone, and they should carry a piece of jade always with them, and, if possible, wear it so that it touches the skin.

FAMOUS PEOPLE BORN UNDER THE NUMBER 2

Thomas Chatterton, the Boy Poet	20th Nov	Represents a	2
Swedenborg	29th Jan.	"	2
Marie Antionette, Queen of France	2nd Nov.	"	2
Gladstone	29th Dec	"	2
Queen Elizabeth of Rumania	29th Dec.	"	2
Sadi Carnot, President of France	11th Aug	"	2
General Boulanger	29th April	"	2
Napoleon III	20th April	"	2
King Victor Emmanuel III	11th Nov.	"	2
Edison	11th Feb.	"	2
David Garrick	20th Feb.	"	2
Lord Curzon of Kedleston	11th Jan.	"	2
Ibsen	20th Mar.	"	2
William Lecky	20th Mar.	"	2
Charles II	29th May	"	2
Sir Edward Elgar	2nd June	"	2
Thomas Hardy	2nd June	"	2
Gluck	2nd July	"	2
President Adams	11th July	"	2
President Harding	2nd Nov.	"	2
President Poincare	20th Aug.	"	2
Paul Bourget	2nd Sept.	"	2
Henry George	2nd Sept.	"	2
Amelia E. Barr	29th Mar.	"	2
Max O'Rell	2nd Mar.	"	2

Eugene Field	2nd Sept.	Represents a	2
Henry George	2nd Sept.	,,	2
Joseph Jefferson	20th Feb.	,,	2
Pope Leo XIII	2nd Mar.	,,	2
Alfred de Musset	11th Nov.	,,	2
Pope Pius X	2nd June	,,	2
Bob Hope	29th May	,,	2
Sophia Loren	20th Sept.	,,	2
Bing Crosby	2nd May	,,	2
Harold Wilson	11th Mar.	,,	2

6. THE SIGNIFICANCE OF NUMBER 3

Symbolically, number 3 stands for the planet Jupiter, a planet which plays a most important role both in Astrology and in all systems of Numerology. Number 3 is the beginning of what may be termed one of the main lines of force that runs right through all the numbers from 3 to 9. It has a special relation to every third in the series, such as 3, 6, 9 and all their additions. These numbers added together in any direction produce a 9 as their final digit, and the 3, 6, 9 people are all sympathetic to one another.

Persons having a 3 for their Birth number are all those who are born on the 3rd, 12th, 21st or 30th in any month, but the number 3 has still more significance if they should be born in what is called the 'period of the 3', from February 19th to March 20th-27th or from November 21st to December 20th-27th.

Number 3 people, like the number 1 individuals, are decidedly ambitious; they are never satisfied by being in subordinate positions; their aim is to rise in the world, to have control and authority over others. They are excellent in the execution of commands; they love order and discipline in all things; they readily obey orders themselves, but they also insist on having their orders obeyed.

Number 3 people often rise to the very highest positions in any business profession or sphere in which they may he found. They often excel in positions of authority in the army and navy in government, and in life generally, and especially in all posts of trust and responsibility, as they are extremely conscientious in carrying out their duties.

Their faults are that they are inclined to be dictatorial, to 'lay down the law' and to insist on carrying out their own ideas. For this reason, they succeed in making many enemies, although they are not quarrelsome.

Number 3 people are singularly proud; they dislike being under an obligation to others; they are also exceptionally independent, and chafe under the least restraint.

Number 3 people should endeavour to carry out their plans and aims on all days that vibrate to their own number, such as on the 3rd, 12th, 21st, and 30th of any month, but more especially when these dates fall in the 'period of the 3' such as from February 19th to March 20th-27th and from the 21st November to December 20th-27th.

The days of the week more 'lucky' for them are Tuesday, Thursday and Friday; Thursday being the most important. These days are especially good if a number forming 3 should fall on it, such as the 3rd, 12th, 21st or 30th and next in order their interchangeable numbers of '6' and '9', such as the 6th, 9th, 15th, 18th, 24th, 27th.

Number 3 people are more in harmony with those born under their own number or under '6' and '9', such as all those who are born on 3rd, 12th, 21st, 30th; 6th, 15th, 24th; 9th, 18th, 27th.

People born under number 3 should wear shades of mauve, violet or purple or some touch of these colours should always be with them and also in their room for these are their lucky colours. All shades of blue, crimson and rose are also favourable to them, but these are more or less secondary 'lucky' colours.

Their 'lucky' stone is the amethyst. They should always have one on their persons, and, if possible, wear it next their skin.

FAMOUS PEOPLE BORN UNDER THE NUMBER 3

King George V	3rd June	Represents a	3
Emperor Frederick of Germany	21st Nov.	”	3
Gambetta of Italy	30th Oct.	”	3
Lord Russell	12th Aug.	”	3
Abraham Lincoln, President,	12th Feb.	”	3
Winston Churchill, M.P.	30th Nov.	”	3
Field-Marshal Lord Roberts, V.C.	30th Sep.	”	3
Rudyard Kipling	30th Dec.	”	3
Sir Arthur Sullivan	12th May	”	3
Sir Charles Hawtrey	21st Sept.	”	3
Lord Beaconsfield	21st Dec.	”	3
Darwin	12th Feb.	”	3
George Pullman	3rd Mar.	”	3
Bishop Heber	21st April	”	3

Sir Alfred Austin	30th May	Represent a	3
Richard Cobden	3rd June	”	3
The Earl of Aberdeen	3rd Aug.	”	3
King Haakon	3rd Aug.	”	3
George IV	12th Aug.	”	3
The First Lord Oxford and Asquith	12th Sept.	”	3
William Cullen Bryant	3rd Nov.	”	3
Mrs. Craigie	3rd Nov.	”	3
Pope Benedict	21st Nov.	”	3
'Mark Twain'	30th Nov.	”	3
President Felix Faure	30th Jan.	”	3
Mendelssohn	3rd Feb.	”	3
Cardinal Newman	21st Feb.	”	3
Dean Swift	30th Nov.	”	3
Voltaire	21st Nov.	”	3
Ramsay MacDonald	12th Oct.	”	3
Joseph Stalin	21st Dec.	”	3
Frank Sinatra	12th Dec.	”	3
John Osborne	12th Dec.	”	3
Henry Moore	30th July	”	3

7. THE SIGNIFICANCE OF NUMBER 4

The number 4 stands in its symbolism for the planet Uranus. It is considered related to the Sun, number 1, and in occultism is written as 4-1.

Number 4 people have a distinct character of their own. They appear to view everything from an opposite angle to everyone else. In an argument they will always take the opposite side, and although not meaning to be quarrelsome, yet they bring about opposition and make a great number of secret enemies who constantly work against them.

They seem quite naturally to take a different view of anything that is presented to their minds. They instinctively rebel against rules and regulations, and if they can have their way they reverse the order of things, even in communities, and governments. They often rebel against constitutional authority and set up new rules and regulations either in domestic or public life. They are inclined to be attracted to social questions and reforms of all kinds, and are very positive and unconventional in their views and opinions.

Number 4 people are all those who are born on the 4th, 13th, 22nd, and 31st in any month; their individuality is still more pronounced if they are born in the Zodiacal period of the Sun and the Moon, namely, between June 21st and July 20th-27th (Moon period) and from 21st July to the end of August (Sun period). Number 4 people do not make friends easily. They seem more attracted to persons born under the numbers 1, 2, 7, and 8. They are seldom as successful in worldly or material matters as people born under the other numbers, and as a rule they are more or less indifferent as to the accumulation of the wealth. If they do acquire money or have it given to them they generally surprise people by the way they employ it or the use they put it to.

They should endeavour to carry out their plans and ideas on all days that have their number 4, such as the 4th, 13th, 22nd, and 31st of any month, but especially so if these dates come in their strong period, from June 21st to July 20th-27th or from 22nd July to the end of August.

The days of the week more fortunate or 'lucky' for them are Saturday, Sunday, and Monday, especially so if their 'own number' should fall on one of these days, such as the 4th, 13th, 22nd or 31st, and next in order their interchageable numbers of 1, 2, 7, such as the 1st, 2nd, 7th, 10th, 11th, 16th, 19th, 20th, 25th, 28th or 29th.

Their chief faults are that they are most highly strung and sensitive, very easily wounded in their feelings, inclined to feel lonely and isolated, and are likely to become despondent and melancholy unless they have achieved success. As a rule they make few real friends, but to the few they have, they are most devoted and loyal, but are always inclined to take the part of 'the under-dog' in any argument or any cause they espouse.

These people should wear what are called' half-shades,' 'half-tones,' or 'electric colours'. 'Electric blues' and 'greys' seem to suit them best of all. Their 'lucky' stone is the sapphire—light or dark, and when they wear this stone it should touch their skin.

FAMOUS PEOPLE BORN UNDER THE NUMBER 4

The Earl of Stafford	13th April	Represents a	4
George Washington	22nd Feb.	"	4
Lord Byron	22nd Jan.	"	4
George Eliot	22nd Nov.	"	4
Lord Baden-Powell of Gilwell	22nd Feb.	"	4
The Queen of Holland	31st Aug.	"	4
Sarah Bernhardt	22nd Oct.	"	4
Thomas Carlyle	4th Dec.	"	4
Faraday	22nd Oct.	"	4
Lord Leighton	4th Dec.	"	4
Prince Charlie	31st Dec.	"	4
Sir Francis Bacon	22nd Jan.	"	4
James Russell Lowell	22nd Feb.	"	4
Haydn	31th April	"	4
Thomas Huxley	4th May	"	4
Alphonse Daudet	13th May	"	4
Sir Arthur Conan Doyle	22nd May	"	4
George III	4th June	"	4
Julian Hawthorne	22nd June	"	4

Rider Haggard	22nd June	Represents a	4
General Goettals	22nd June	”	4
Nathaniel Hawthorne	4th July	”	4
Emma Eames	13th Aug.	”	4
Archbishop Corrigan	13th Aug.	”	4
Ex-Sultan Abdul Hamid	22nd Sept.	”	4
Saint Augustine	13th Nov.	”	4
Heinrich Heine	13th Dec.	”	4
Immanuel Kant	22nd April	”	4
Sir Issac Pitman	4th Jan.	”	4
Pope Pius IX	13th May	”	4
Russell Sage	4th Aug.	”	4
Schubert	31st Jan.	”	4
Sir Arthur Sullivan	13th May	”	4
Richard Wagner	22nd May	”	4
Sir Hamilton Harty	4th Dec.	”	4
Laurence Olivier	22nd May	”	4
Maria Callas	4th Dec.	”	4
Charles de Gaulle	22nd Nov.	”	4
Yehudi Menuhin	22nd April	”	4

8. THE SIGNIFICANCE OF NUMBER 5

The number 5 stands for the planet Mercury, and is versatile and mercurial in all its characteristics. Number 5 people are all those who are born on the 5th, 14th, and 23rd in any month, but their characteristics are still more marked if they are born in what is called the 'period of the 5,' which is from May 21st to June 20th-27th, and from August 21st to September 20th-27th.

Number 5 people make friends easily and get on with persons born under almost any other number, but their best friends are those who are born under their own number, such as the 5th, 14th, and 23rd of any month.

Number 5 people are mentally very highly strung. They live on their nerves and appear to crave for excitement. They are quick in thought and decisions, and impulsive in their actions. They detest any plodding kind of work and seem naturally to drift into all methods of making money quickly. They have a keen sense of making money by inventions and new ideas. They are born speculators, prone to Stock Exchange transactions, and generally are willing and ready to run risks in all they undertake.

They have the most wonderful elasticity of character. They rebound quickly from the heaviest blow; nothing seems to affect them for very long; like their symbol, quicksilver, represented by Mercury, the blows of Fate leave no indentations on their character. If they are by nature good they remain so; if bad, not all the preaching in the world will have the slightest effect on them.

Number 5 people should endeavour to carry out their plans and aims on all days that fall under their 'own number' such as the 5th, 14th or 23rd of any month, but more especially when these dates fall in the 'period of the 5,' namely from May 21st to June 20th-27th or from the 21st August to September 20th—27th.

The days of the week more fortunate or 'lucky' for them are Wednesday and Friday, especially if their 'own number' falls on one of these days.

Their greatest drawback is that they exhaust their nervous strength to such an extent that they often fall victims to nervous breakdowns of the worst kind, and under any mental tension they easily become irritable and quick-tempered, unable to 'suffer fools gladly.'

Their 'lucky' colours are all shades of light grey, white, and glistening materials, but just as they can make friends with people born under all kinds of numbers, so they can wear all shades of colours, but by far the best for them are light shades, and they should wear dark colours as rarely as possible.

Their 'lucky' stone is the diamond. They can also wear other glittering or shimmering things and also ornaments made of platinum or silver. If possible, they should wear a diamond set in platinum next their skin.

FAMOUS PEOPLE BORN UNDER THE NUMBER 5

St. Louis of France	23rd May	Represents a	5
Louis XVI	23rd Aug.	,,	5
Empress Eugenie	5th May	,,	5
H.M. King George VI	14th Dec.	,,	5
H.R.H The Duke of Windsor	23rd June	,,	5
Samuel Pepys	23rd Feb.	,,	5
Sir Hiram Maxim	5th Feb.	,,	5
Lord Lister	5th April	,,	5
T.P. O'Connor, M.P.	5th Oct.	,,	5
Jean de Reske	14th Jan.	,,	5
Sir Henry Bessemer	14th Mar.	,,	5
Humbert I of Italy	14 Mar.	,,	5
Shakespeare	23rd April	,,	5
Thomas Hood	23rd May	,,	5
Chateaubriand	14th Sept.	,,	5
Benedict Arnold	14th Jan.	,,	5
Barnum	5th July	,,	5
Erard	5th April	,,	5
Handel	23rd Feb.	,,	5
Fahrenheit	14th May	,,	5
Josephine, Queen of France	23rd June	,,	5

Karl Marx	5th May	Represents a	5
Mesmer	23rd May	"	5
Sir Gilbert Parker	23rd Nov.	"	5
Cardinal Richelieu	5th Sept.	"	5
W.T. Stead	5th Feb.	"	5
Talleyrand	14th Feb.	"	5
Neil Armstrong	5th Aug.	"	5
Dwight Eisenhower	14th Oct.	"	5
Albert Einstein	14th Mar.	"	5

9. THE SIGNIFICANCE OF NUMBER 6

The number 6 stands in symbolism for the planet Venus. Persons having 6 as their birth number are all those who are born on the 6th, 15th or 24th, of any month, but they are more especially influenced by this number if they are born in what is called the 'House of 6th, which is from 20th April to May 20th-27th, and from the 21st September to October 20th-27th.

As a rule all number 6 people are extremely magnetic; they attract others to them, and they are loved and often worshipped by those under them. They are very determined in carrying out their plans, and may, in fact, be deemed obstinate and unyielding, except when they themselves become deeply attached; in such a case they become devoted slaves to those they love.

Although number 6 people are considered influenced by the planet Venus, yet as a rule theirs is more the 'mother love' than the sensual. They lean to the romantic and ideal in all matters of the affections. In some ways they take very strongly after the supposed qualities of Venus, in that they love beautiful things, they make most artistic homes, are fond of rich colours , also paintings, statuary, and music.

If rich they are most generous to art and artists, they love to entertain their friends and make everyone happy about them, but the things they cannot stand are discord and jealousy.

When roused by anger they will brook no opposition, and will fight to the death for whatever person or cause they espouse or out of their sense of duty.

The number 6 people have got the power of making more friends than any other class, with the exception of the number 5, but especially so with all persons born under the vibration of the 3, 6, 9 or all their series.

Their most important days in the week are Tuesday, Thursday, and Friday, and especially so if a number of 3, 6 or 9, such as the 3rd, 6th, 9th, 12th, 18th, 21st, 24th, 27th or 30th, should fall on one of those days.

They should endeavour to carry out their plans and aims on all dates that fall under their 'own number,' such as the 6th, 15th or 24th, of any month, but more especially when these dates fall in the 'period of the 6,' namely, between April 20th and May 20th-27th or from the 21st of September to October 20th-27th.

Their 'lucky' colours are all shades of blue, from the lightest to the darkest, and also all shades of rose or pink, but they should avoid wearing black or dark purple.

Their 'lucky' stone is the turquoise, and, if possible, they should wear at least a piece of turquoise matrix, next their skin. Emeralds are also 'lucky' for the number 6 people.

FAMOUS PEOPLE BORN UNDER THE NUMBER 6

Queen Victoria	24th May	Represents a	6
Napoleon I	15th Aug.	”	6
Frederic the Great	24th Jan.	”	6
Duke of Marlborough	24th May	”	6
Emperor Maximilian of Mexico	6th July	”	6
Henry VI	6th Dec.	”	6
Oliver Cromwell	24th April	”	6
Cecil Rhodes	6th July	”	6
Joan of Arc	6th Jan.	”	6
Admiral Lord Jellicoe	6th Dec.	”	6
President Taft	15th Sept.	”	6
Sir Walter Scott	6th Dec.	”	6
Sir Henry Irving	6th Feb.	”	6
Joseph Choate	24th Jan.	”	6
Susan B. Anthony	15th Feb.	”	6
Michael Angelo	6th Mar.	”	6
Elizabeth Browing	6th Mar.	”	6
Henry Ward Beecher	24th June	”	6
President Diaz	15th Sept.	”	6
Sir William Herschel	15th Nov.	”	6
Grace Darling	24th Nov.	”	6
Warren Hastings	6th Dec.	”	6
King George I	24th Dec.	”	6
John Knox	24th Nov.	”	6

Moliere	15th Jan.	Represents a	6
Max Muller	6th Dec.	,,	6
Daniel O'Connell	6th Aug.	,,	6
Count de Paris	24th Aug.	,,	6
Admiral Peary	6th May	,,	6
Sir Arthur Pinero	24th May	,,	6
Rembrandt	15th July	,,	6
Alfred Tennyson	6th Aug.	,,	6
George Westinghouse	6th Oct.	,,	6
P.G. Wodehouse	15th Oct.	,,	6
Gamal Nasser	15th Jan.	,,	6
Alexander Fleming	6th Aug.	,,	6

10. THE SIGNIFICANCE OF NUMBER 7

The number 7 is symbolic of for the planet Neptune, and represents all persons born under the 7, namely those who are born on the 7th, 16th or 25th of any month, but more especially influences such person if they were born from the 21st June to July 20th-27th, the period of the Zodiac called the 'House of the Moon.' The planet Neptune has always been considered as associated with the Moon, and, it being the part of the Zodiac I have mentioned earlier, is also called the First House of Water.

Now, as the number of the Moon is always given as 2, it gives ample explanation as to why the number 7 people have number 2 as their secondary number and get on well and make friends easily with all those born under the Moon numbers, namely, the 2nd, 11th, 20th and 29th of any month, especially so if they are also born in the 'House of the Moon,' from the 21st of June to the end of July.

People born under number 7, namely, on the 7th, 16th or 25th of any month, are very independent, original, and have strongly marked individuality. At heart they love change and travel, being restless in their natures. If they have the means of gratifying their desire they visit foreign countries and become keenly interested in the affairs of far-off lands. They devour books on travel and have a wide universal knowledge of the world at large.

They often make extremely good writers, painters or poets, but in everything they do, they sooner or later show a peculiar philosophical outlook on life that tinges all their work.

As a class they care little about the material things of life; they often become rich by their original ideas or methods of business. If they are rich, they are likely to make huge contributions from their wealth in charity and donations. The women born under this number generally marry well, as they are always anxious about the future, and feel that they need some rock to rest, lest the waters of Fate sweep them away.

The number 7 people have good ideas about business or rather their plans are good if they will only carry them out. They have usually a keen desire to travel and read a great deal about far-off countries. If they can they will become interested in matters concerning the sea, and in trade or business; they often become merchants, exporters, and importers, dealing with foreign countries, and owners or captains of ships.

Number 7 people have very peculiar ideas about religion. They dislike to follow the beaten track; they create a religion of their own, but one that appeals to the imagination and based on the mysterious.

These people usually have remarkable dreams and a great leaning to occultism; they have the gift of intuition, clairvoyance, and a peculiar quieting magnetism of their own that has great influence over others.

Number 7 people should endeavour to carry out their plans and aims on all days that fall under their 'own number,' such as the 7th, 16th or 25th of any month, but more especially when these dates fall in the 'period of the 7,' namely, from the 21st June to July 20th-27th and less strongly from that date to the end of August.

The days of the week more fortunate or 'lucky' for them are the same as for the number 2 people, namely, Sunday, Monday, especially if their 'own number' or their interchangeable numbers 1,2,4 such as the 1st, 2nd, 4th, 10th, 11th, 13th, 19th, 20th, 22nd, 28th, 29th or 31st falls on one of these days.

Their 'lucky' colours are all shades of green, pale shades, as also white and yellow. They should avoid all heavy dark colours as much as possible.

Their 'lucky' stones are moonstones, cat's-eyes, and pearls, and if possible, they should wear a moonstone or a piece of moss against their skin.

FAMOUS PEOPLE BORN UNDER THE NUMBER 7

Queen Elizabeth 1	7th Sept.	Represents a	7
Louis XIV	16th Sept.	”	7
Empress Charlotte of Mexico	7th June	”	7
Lord Rosebery	7th May	”	7
Lord Balfour	25th July	”	7
Admiral Earl Beatty	16th Jan.	”	7
Bonar Law, M.P.	16th Sept.	”	7
Charles Dickens	7th Feb.	”	7

Sir Joshua Reynolds	16th July	Represents a	7
Oscar Wilde	16th Oct.	”	7
Ernst Haeckel	16th Feb.	”	7
Camille Flammarion	25th Feb.	”	7
Prince Imperial	16th Mar.	”	7
Sir John Franklin	16th April	”	7
Robert Browning	7th May	”	7
Ralph Waldo Emerson	25th June	”	7
Dean Farrar	7th Aug.	”	7
Bret Harte	25th Aug.	”	7
Philip D. Armour	16th May	”	7
Andrew Carnegie	25th Nov.	”	7
Sir Isaac Newton	25th Dec.	”	7
Rousseau	16th April	”	7
Sardou	7th Sept.	”	7
De Witt Talmage	7th Jan.	”	7
William Wordsworth	7th April	”	7
Noel Coward	16th Dec.	”	7
David Frost	7th April	”	7
Pablo Picasso	25th Oct.	”	7
Billy Graham	7th Nov.	”	7

11. THE SIGNIFICANCE OF NUMBER 8

The number 8 stands for the planet Saturn. This number influences all persons born on the 8th, 17th or 26th in any month, but still more so if their birthday comes between 21st December and 26th January, which period is called the House of Saturn (Positive), and from 26th January to February 19th-26th, the period called the House of Saturn (Negative).

These people are invariably much misunderstood in their lives, and perhaps for this reason they feel intensely lonely at heart. They have deep and very intense nature, great strength of individuality; they generally play some important role on life's stage, but usually one which is fatalistic or as the instrument of Fate for others.

If at all religious they go to extremes and are fanatics in their zeal. In any cause they take up, they attempt to carry it through in spite of all arguments or opposition, and in doing so they generally make bitter and relentless enemies.

They often appear cold and undemonstrative, though in reality they have warm heart towards the oppressed of all classes; but they hide their feelings and allow people to think just what they please.

These number 8 people are either great successes or great failures; there appears to be no happy medium in their case. If ambitious, they generally aim for public life or government responsibility of some kind, and often hold very high positions involving great sacrifice on their part. It is not, however, from a worldly standpoint, a fortunate number to be born under, and such persons are often called greatest sorrows, losses, and humiliations.

The 'lucky' colours for people born under the 8 are all shades of dark grey, black, dark blue, and purple. If number 8 persons were to dress in light colours they would look awkward, as if something is wrong with them.

The number 8 being a Saturn number, Saturday is their most important day, but as number 4 has an influence on Sunday and in a secondary way on Monday, the number 8 people will find Saturday, Sunday, and Monday as their most important days.

Number 8 people should endeavour to carry out their plans and aims all days that fall under their 'own number,' such as the 8th, 17th or 26th in any month, but more especially so when these dates fall in the 'period of the 8,' namely, from December 21st to January 20th-27th, and from that date to February 19th-26th; also if these dates fall on a Saturday, Sunday or Monday or on their interchangeable number, which is 4, such as the 4th, 13th, 22nd or 31st.

Their 'lucky' stones are the amethyst and the dark toned sapphire, also the black pearl or the black diamond and if possible they should always wear one of these against their skin.

The number 8 is a difficult number to explain. It represents two worlds, the material and the spiritual. It is in fact, like two circles just touching together. It is composed of two equal numbers : 4 and 4.

From the earliest ages it has been associated with the symbol of an irrevocable Fate, both in connection with the lives of individuals or nations. In Astrology it stands for Saturn, which is also called the Planet of Fate.

One side of the nature of this number represents upheaval, revolution, anarchy, waywardness, and eccentricities of all kinds.

The other side represents philosophic thought, a strong leaning towards occult studies, religious devotion, concentration of purpose, zeal for any cause espoused and a fatalistic outlook colouring all actions.

All persons who have the number 8 clearly associated with their lives feel that they are distinct and different from their fellows. At heart they are lonely; they are misunderstood, and they seldom reap the reward for the good they may do while they are living. After their death they are often extolled, their works praised, and lasting tributes offered in their memory.

Those on the lower plane generally come into conflict with human justice and have some tragic ending to their lives. Those on the higher plane carry their misunderstood motives and lay bare the tragedy of their souls before Divine Justice.

To distinguish in which of these two classes a number 8 person falls, one must find by the comparison of their 'fadic' numbers if they are completely dominated by the recurrence of 8 in the principal events of their lives or if some other equally powerful number such as the 1, 3 or 6 series, more or less balance the sequel of events registered under the 8 and all its series.

If the latter is the case, one may be sure that by the long series of reincarnations they have passed through, they have paid the price in some former state, and are now passing towards the higher, where they will be rewarded with the Divine Justice. If on the contrary, we find that the person is completely dominated by the number 8, recurring in important events or if instead of 8 the nearly equally fatalistic number of 4 is continually recurring, we may then be sure that the person is placed in the vicinity of one of those strange playthings of Fate with the possibilities that tragedy may be interwoven in their Destiny.

In the more ordinary tragedies of every day life, we can find an illuminating example in the life and execution of Crippen, whose principal actions were singularly influenced by the terrible combination of the 8 and the 4. Looking back over his career, and especially the events which led up to his paying that terrible forfeit at the hands of the law, one will find these numbers associated in the most dramatic way with this man's life, as illustrated by the following facts.

The figures of the year he was born in (1862), if added together, produce an 8 (17 equals 1 plus 7 which equals 8). He was born on the 26th January or 2 plus 6 equals 8. His wife was not seen alive after a dinner with him on the 31st January, which is a 4, and the month of January is itself called the House of Saturn, whose number is an 8. He made his statement to Inspector Drew (which was later to be used as an overwhelming evidence against him) on the 8th of July. The human remains were found in the cellar on 13th July, which again makes the number 4. In order to escape he chose the name 'Robinson,' which has, strange to say, 8 letters in it. He was recognised on board of the Montrose on the 22nd July, which again equals a 4. The name of the ship he chose to leave Europe—the Montrose was 8 lettered, and the ship that brought him back to his doom, the Megantic, was also composed of 8 letters. He was arrested, as this ship reached Canada, on the morning of 31st July, which again equals 4.

His trial finished on Saturday, 22nd October, which again adds to 4, and October being the month of 'the detriment of Saturn' stands for 8. The occult number by which Saturday is also designated is also an 8.

His execution was fixed for the 8th November. His appeal was heard and refused on Saturday, 5th November. The 5 amounted to 8, as it is the symbol of Saturday, the numbers, if added up makes the figure 13, which again is an equivalent of 4.

When his appeal failed, the date of execution was changed to 23rd November. The addition of 2 and 3 gives a 5, and the division of the Zodiac which represents this portion of November is designated as 3; and this 3, if added to the date (the 23rd), makes the figure 26, which if added (2 plus 6) again makes 8. Or if the 3 were to be added to the number of 23 we would get 26 or the 8. From time immemorial, in occult studies, number 8 is considered as the 'symbol of human justice.' Lastly, when Crippen's 'Key numbers,' the 4 and 8 came together, it was the fatal year of his life. He was 48 years old when executed.

It is not my province to judge or condemn this unfortunate being. Crippen, in any case, suffered as few men have been called upon to suffer; but I may add that the combination of such numbers as 4 and 8 as the 'Key numbers' in any life, can force an individual terribly under the influence of Fate, and one especially unfortunate through his or her affections.

I have followed out many cases of people having similar 'Key numbers,' and in every case they seem sooner or later to come into conflict with what the 8 represents, namely, the symbol of 'human justice'. They are generally condemned, even in ordinary social life, by the weight of circumstantial evidence, and they usually die with their secret, as if appealing to the Divine Justice the world beyond, challenging the sentence of 'human justice'.

The occult symbol of 8 has from time immemorial been represented by the figure of Justice with a Sword pointing upwards and a Balance or Scales in the left hand. There are many curious things in history as regards this number. The Greeks called it the number of Justice on account of its equal divisions of equally even numbers.

The Jews practised circumcision on the 8th day after birth. At their Feast of Dedication they kept 8 candles burning, and this Feast lasted 8 days. Eight prophets were descended from Rahab. There were 8 sects of Pharisees. Noah was the 8th direct descendant of Adam.

The strange number of three eights (888) is considered by students of Occultism as the number of Jesus Christ in His aspect as the Redeemer of the world. Curiously enough, the addition of 888 makes 24 and 2 plus 4 gives the 6 which is the number of Venus, the representative of Love.

This number 888 given to Christ is in direct opposition to 666 which Revelation says is the number of the Beast or the number of Man. The numbers 666 if added together gives 18 (1 plus 8 equals 9). This 9 is the number of Mars, the symbol of war, destruction, and force, which is decidedly in opposition to the 6 which is the symbol of Love.

REMARKABLE PEOPLE BORN UNDER THE 8

Mary I of England	17th Feb.	Represents an	8
King Albert of Belgium	8th April	”	8
Queen Mary	26th May	”	8
Alfonso XIII of Spain	17th May	”	8
Joseph Chamberlain	8th July	”	8
George Bernard Shaw	26th July	”	8
David Lloyd George	17th Jan.	”	8
Prince Albert	26th Aug.	”	8
Admiral Dewey	26th Dec.	”	8
Bernadotte, King of Sweden	26th Jan.	”	8
Colonel Cody	26th Feb.	”	8
Wilkie Collins	8th Jan.	”	8
Louis Conde of France	8th Sept.	”	8
Sir Humphry Davy	17th Dec.	”	8
Gounod	17th June	”	8
Jenner	17th May	”	8
La Fontaine	8th July	”	8
Mary, Queen of Scots	8th Dec.	”	8
Sir John Millais	8th June	”	8
General von Moltke	26th Oct.	”	8
Pierpont-Morgan	17th April	”	8
Richard I	8th Sept.	”	8
J.D. Rockefeller	8th July	”	8
Jules Verne	8th Feb.	”	8
John Wesley	17th June	”	8
Christian Barnard	8th Oct.	”	8
Elizabeth Taylor	17th Feb.	”	8
Rudolf Nureyev	17th Mar.	”	8
Compton Mackenzie	17th Jan.	”	8

12. THE SIGNIFICANCE OF NUMBER 9

The number 9 stands as a symbol for the planet Mars. This number influences all persons born on the 9th, 18th, and 27th of any month, but still more so if their birthday falls in the period between March 21st and April 19th-26th (called the House of Mars Positive) or in the period between October 21st and November 20th-27th (called the House of Mars Negative).

Number 9 people are fighters at core, in all, they make an attempt on other's life. They usually have difficult times in their early years, but generally they are, in the end, successful by their grit, strong will, and determination. In character, they are hasty in temper, impulsive, independent and desire to be their own masters. When the number 9 is noticed to be more than usually dominant in the dates and events of their lives there are improved chances of their making great enemies, causing strife and opposition wherever they may be, and they are often wounded or killed either in warfare or in the battle of life.

They have great courage and make excellent soldiers or leaders in any cause they espouse. Their foolhardiness and impulsiveness in word and action turns to be of great danger to them. They are also peculiarly prone to accidents from fire and explosions and rarely get through life without injury from such causes. As a result they undergo many operations at the hands of a surgeon. They usually experience many quarrels and strifes in their home life, either with their own relations or with the family they marry into. They strongly resent criticism, and even when not conceited, they have always a good opinion of themselves, brooking no interference with their plans. They like to be 'looked up to' and recognised as 'the head of the house'.

They are resourceful and excellent in organisation, but they must have the fullest control; if not, they lose heart and stand aside and let things go to pieces. For affection and sympathy they will do almost anything, and the men of this number can be made the greatest fool if some clever woman gets pulling at their heartstrings.

As a rule they get on with persons whose birth date is one of the series of 3, 6 or 9, such as those born on the 3rd, 6th, 9th, 12th, 15th, 18th, 21st, 24th, 27th or 30th of any month. All these numbers are in harmonious vibration to the number 9 people.

This number 9 has some very curious properties. It is the only number in calculation that, multiplied by any number, always reproduces itself, as for example 9 times 2 is 18, and 8 plus 1 becomes again the 9, and so on with it; every multiples.

It is, perhaps, not uninteresting to notice that at the 9th day the ancients buried their dead; at the 9th hour Christ died on the Cross and the Romans held a feast in memory of their dead every 9th year. In some of the Hebrew writings it is taught that God descended to this earth 9 times—firstly, in the Garden of Eden; secondly, during the confusion of tongues at Babel; thirdly, at the destruction of Sodom and Gomorrah; fourthly, to Moses at Horeb; fifthly, at Sinai when the Ten Commandments were given; sixthly, to Balaam; seventhly, to Elisha; eighthly, in the Tabernacle; ninthly, in the Temple at Jerusalem. And it is taught that at the 10th coming this earth will pass away and a new one will be created. Both the First and Second Temples of the Jews were destroyed on the 9th day of the Jewish month called Ab. On the 9th day of Ab, Jews who follow their religion cannot wear the Talith and Phylacteries until the Sun has set.

There are so many curious things connected with the number 9 that it would not be possible to deal with one-half of them in a book of this description. This number is supposed to be a fortunate one to be born under, provided one controls it and is not carried away by the excesses of temper and violence which is also represented by it.

The 'lucky' colours for persons born under the number 9 are all shades of crimson or red, also all rose tones and pink. Their most important days in the week are Tuesday, Thursday, and Friday, but more especially Tuesday (called Mars Day). Their 'lucky' stones are the ruby, garnet and bloodstone, and they should always wear one of these stones.

Number 9 people should endeavour to carry out their plans and aims on all days that fall under their 'own number,' such as the 9th, 18th or 27th in any month, but more especially when these dates fall in the 'period of the 9,' between March 21st and April 19th-26th or from October 21st to November 20th-27th; and also when 9th, 18th or 27th alls on their 'own day,' as mentioned above or on one of their interchageable numbers like 3 and 6, such as the 3rd, 6th 12th, 15th, 21st, 24th, and 30th.

For all purposes of occult calculation the numbers 7 and 9 are considered the most important of all. The 7 has always been understood to relate to the spiritual plane, acting as the God or creative force on the Earth, and being creative, it is the uplifting 'urge' towards the higher development of the spiritual in humanity. The 9 on the contrary, being, the representative of the planet Mars in the Planetary World, is the number of physical force in every form, and consequently stands in relation to the material.

When this explanation is carefully considered it throws an illuminating light on the mysterious text in Revelation, chapter xiii, verse 18 : "Here is wisdom. Let him that hath understanding, count the number of the beast, for it is the number of man, and his number is 666."

This strange text has puzzled the theological mind for centuries, yet if you will take the trouble to add 666 together you will get 18, and 1 plus 8 gives you the figure 9, which in turn represent the 9 Planets of our Solar System, the 9 numbers upon which man builds all his calculations, and beyond which he cannot go except by continual repetition of the numbers is 1to 9.

Number '666' producing the 'spirit number' 9 (as explained earlier) is therefore , in all truth as Revelation states, 'the number of man.' The hidden meaning of this number is one of the greatest secrets of occultism, and has been concealed in a thousand ways, just as the cryptic text in Revelation has hidden it for centuries from the minds of the theologians.

The number 9 representing man and everything to do with the physical and material plane, is the number of force, energy, destruction, and war in its most dominant quality. In its relation to ordinary life it denotes energy, ambition, leadership, dominion. It represents iron, the metal from which the weapons of warfare are made , and the planet Mars which in accordance with Astrology is the Ruler of the Zodiacal Sign Aries which governs England. This symbolism was evidently well known to Shakespeare who wrote, 'England, thou seat of Mars.'

The number 9 is an emblem of matter that can never be destroyed, so the number 9 when multiplied by any number always reproduces itself, no matter what the extent of the number is that has been employed.

The Novendiale was a fast in the Roman Catholic church to avert calamities, and from this came the Roman Catholic system of Neuvaines.

In Freemasonry there is an order of 'Nine Elected Knights,' and in the working of this order 9 roses, 9 lights, and 9 knocks must be used. All ancient races encouraged a fear towards number 9, and all its multiples.

The number 9 is considered a fortunate number to be born under, provided the man or woman does not ask for a peaceful or monotonous life, and can control their nature in not making enemies.

REMARKABLE PEOPLE BORN UNDER THE NUMBER 9

Kaiser Wilhelm	27th Jan.	Represents a	9
King Edward VII	9th Nov.	"	9
Sir Evelyn Wood, V.C.	9th Feb.	"	9
President Theodore Roosevelt	27th Oct.	"	9
President Grover Cleveland	18th Mar.	"	9
Lord Carson	9th Feb.	"	9
Sam Gompers	27th Jan.	"	9
Eyrnest Renan	27th Feb.	"	9
President Ulysses Grant	27th April	"	9
Sir James Barrie	9th May	"	9
Julia Ward Howe	27th May	"	9
Jay Gould	27th May	"	9
Elizabeth, Empress of Austria	18th Aug.	"	9
Franz Josef, Emperor of Austria	18th Aug.	"	9
Fredrick III of Germany	19th Oct.	"	9
Kepler	27th Oct.	"	9
Louis Kossuth	27th April	"	9
Leopold II, of Belgium	9th April	"	9
Nicholas II, of Russia	18th May	"	9
Paganini	18th Feb.	"	9
Whitelaw Reid	27th Oct.	"	9
George Stephenson	9th June	"	9
Edward Heath	9th July	"	9
Richard Nixon	9th Jan.	"	9
Margot Fonteyn	18th May	"	9
Marlene Dietrich	27th Dec.	"	9
Greta Garbo	18th Sept.	"	9
Peter Sellers	18th Sept.	"	9

13. THE OCCULT SYMBOLISM OF 'COUMPOUND' NUMBERS

I am now going to put before my readers one of the most amazing systems comprised in the occult calculations of names and numbers that it has been my good fortune to elucidate. This system, which has never before been made public on the lines I am going to present it, will be, of inestimable value to those who may care to follow the rules I shall give.

I feel sure, from long experience, that the occult philosophy I am now about to pass on will be of the greatest practical utility to every man or woman, who wishes for aid in the hard struggle for existence that is, alas, the fate of so many sons and daughters of humanity.

Shakespeare, the Prince of Philosophers, whose thoughts will adorn English literature for all time, laid down the well-known axiom : "There is a tide in the affairs of men which, taken at the flood, leads on to fortune." The question has been asked again and again — Is there some means of knowing when the moment has come *to take the tide at the flood ?*

My answer to this question is, that the great Architect of the Universe, with His Infinite Wisdom created all things in such harmony of design that He endowed the human mind with some part of that omnipotent knowledge which is the attribute of the Divine Mind, the Creator of all beings. It is this desire for knowledge implanted in the mind of humanity that places mankind above the animal creation, and makes men and women as 'gods' in their desire 'to know'.

We are told that Solomon, the King asked for the endowment of Wisdom, the greatest gift that God could give him, and in the ancient Hebrew of the Book of Solomon we can yet read his inspiring words :

> *I thank Thee, O Great Creator of the Universe, that Thou has taught me the secrets of the planets, that I mayst know the Times and Seasons of Things, the secrets of men's hearts, their thoughts, and the nature of their being. Thou gavest unto me this knowledge which is the foundation of all my Wisdom.*

It is these self-same 'Secrets of the planets' that I have endeavoured to teach in these pages. I now ask my readers to give their attention and concentration to the following system which I will put as briefly and in as clear language as possible.

To find the exact day in any month of the year whose vibration will be favourable or in other words 'lucky' to any individual, the simplest rule is to work out by the following table the occult number produced by the letters of their name.

This ancient Chaldean and Hebrew alphabet sets out the number or value of each letter. It is the best system I know for this purpose; its origin is lost in antiquity, but it is believed that it was originated by the Chaldeans, who were masters in all magical arts, and by them passed to the Hebrews.

It will be seen that there is no number 9 given in the following alphabets, for the simple reason that those ancient masters of Occultism knew that in the 'Highest Sphere' the number 9 represents the nine lettered name of God, and for this reason no single letter was ascribed to it.

If, however, the letters in a name should total up and produce the number 9, the meaning of it is the same as the one I set out in the previous chapter dealing with the number 9, and for the compound numbers of the 9 such as the 18, 27, etc.

A	=	1	G	=	3	N	=	5	T	=	4
B	=	2	H	=	5	O	=	7	U	=	6
C	=	3	I orJ	=	1	P	=	8	V	=	6
D	=	4	K	=	2	Q	=	1	W	=	6
E	=	5	L	=	3	R	=	2	X	=	5
F	=	8	M	=	4	S	=	3	Y	=	1
									Z	=	7

The next important question to be answered is—should all the Christian and Surnames be added together to find the last digit or number?

The answer is that it is the most used Christian and Surname that must be added together to give the Key number; when the Surname is more used or more in evidence than the Christian name, then it is taken to give the key number.

In a book of this description I have the space to give illustrations of a few well-known names only. One I will take was always spoken of as Lloyd George the other an Ex-Prime Minister of England simply known by the name Baldwin.

The names Lloyd George and Baldwin, if transcribed into numbers are as follows :

						B	=	2
			G	=	3	A	=	1
L =		3	E	=	5	L	=	3
L =		3	O	=	7	D	=	4
O =		7	R	=	2	W	=	6
Y =		1	G	=	3	I	=	1
D =		4	E	=	5	N	=	5
		18 = 9			25 = 7			22 = 4

In Lloyd George's case, the word Lloyd alone produces the single number of 9, which as I have previously explained, is connected with people who have to fight hard with circumstances in their early lives and who, if they rise to positions of authority in nations, are often the cause of wars (as with Lloyd George) or play an active part in them.

The word George in itself produces the single number of 7. This is also, as I have previously explained, a magnetic number, and favourable if used by itself. In this case, however, the two names are never used by itself. In this case, however the two names are never used alone, but always together, as Lloyd George. Now add the two single numbers of each name together—7 plus 9 and you get the compound number of 16, the occult symbolism of which is a 'Shattered Citadel' of 'Lightning-struck Tower.' A full description of compound numbers will be found later in these pages.

If, however, the word David were added it would produce another 7, and if the name David Lloyd George was employed in continuous use instead of Lloyd George, the addition of the 7 for the word David would make the total of the three names to number 23, which, as will be seen in Chapter 14 dealing with the meaning of the compound numbers, is considered a fortunate number.

However, by some hidden law of destiny over which man has no control, he became known and called as Lloyd George, and so his name foreshadowed that he would one day in his marvellous career fulfil the symbolism of 'a Shattered Citadel' or 'a Lightning-struck Tower.'

The Ex-Prime Minister due to some unknown reasons was popularly known amongst his political followers and the general public by the name of Baldwin. This name as you will notice, totals up to 22, and in its single figure to 4.

The number 4, as I explained earlier, is not considered to be a fortunate number as people under it are usually misunderstood. They work hard and strive earnestly to carry out their ideas, but their plans usually meet with great opposition.

Taking again these two well-known public leaders for another illustration, I now come to the most curious side of this study of numerology, namely, that the 'compound' numbers have an *extraordinary meaning of their own*, which throws an added light on the mysterious connection they have in the still deeper side of occultism as applied to people's names.

Taking again the name Lloyd George, we find the first word 'Lloyd' gives the 'compound' number 18. In occult symbolism this number is represented as 'a rayed moon from which blood is dropping like rain; in a field below a wolf and a dog are catching drops of blood in their opened mouth.'

Taking the word George, the 'compound' number is 25. In symbolism this number is classed as 'a number of strength gained by experience and ultimate gain through strife.'

The conclusion therefore is that if Lloyd George had become known to the world plainly as George he would have retained to the end the high position he had gained.

Lloyd George was born on January 17th; he was therefore by his birth a number 8 man, which is unfortunately not in harmonious vibration with his name number, and further, being an 8, increases the fatalistic indications given by the number of his name that is 16.

The 'compound' number of 22, made by the name Baldwin, in the same occult symbolism of number is favourable from a purely worldly sense, as a leader of men. The single number of a name, it must be remembered, represents the man or woman as they appear to be. The 'double' or 'compound' number represents the hidden forces that use the man or woman as their instrument. The number 22 symbolises a 'good man blinded by the folly of others, with a knapsack on his back full of errors ; he offers no defence against a ferocious tiger who is biting him.'

I have, of course, no political leanings in any direction; I merely am your mentor in these studies.

Sketch your world exactly as it goes—without offence—to friends or foes. I have only quoted the symbolism given to these numbers since the most ancient times.

SIR AUSTEN CHAMBERLAIN

As Sir Austen Chamberlain was generally spoken of as Austen Chamberlain, his numbers are as follows:

A	=	1		C	=	3
U	=	6		H	=	5
S	=	3		A	=	1
T	=	4		M	=	4
E	=	5		B	=	2
N	=	5		E	=	5
				R	=	2
		24 = 6		L	=	3
				A	=	1
				I	=	1
				N	=	5
						32 = 5

Both the single numbers and the compound numbers in this name are singluarly fortunate, especially if used separately, as I have explained in a previous chapter. The number 6 is usually found associated with persons who rise to high positions of authority—especially in political life.

The compound number 24 is also favourable, and in occult symbolism it is put down as a number that brings 'the assistance and association of people of high rank, and gain through such association.'

The single number of 5, as in the name Chamberlain is, as I have mentioned earlier, a 'lucky' number, especially for those who have in their lives a large element of risk, change and speculation involving in their career; while the compound number of 32 is also given in occult symbolism as a magical number and is associated with what is called 'the Paths of Wisdom.'

His title of 'Sir' produces the number 6, again a favourable number, and if we now add the single numbers of all the three together, we get 6 plus 6 plus 5 which equals to 17, a comound number whose occult symbolism is curiously enough the 8-pointed Star of Venus, a symbol of Peace and Love, which is peculiarly suitable for the career of a man who made superhuman efforts towards bringing peace between nations at Locarno. If, however, he was only known as Austen Chamberlain, the total of these two words produce the number 11, which, as my readers will see later on, gives warning of 'hidden dangers, trial and treachery from others.'

Sir Austen Chamberlain was born on October 16th. Neither the single number of 7 nor the compound are in harmonious vibration with the number of his name. This was not a favourable promise for a successful ending of his career, as is explained later on in these pages.

RAMSAY MACDONALD

We will take the first Labour Prime Minister of England for our next illustration. His numbers are as follows :

R	=	2	M	=	4
A	=	1	A	=	1
M	=	4	C	=	3
S	=	3	D	=	4
A	=	1	O	=	7
Y	=	1	N	=	5
		–––	A	=	1
		12 = 3	L	=	3
			D	=	4
					–––
					32 = 5

It will be seen that the name Ramsay produces 3 as its simple number and 12 for its compound number.

As I have explained earlier in this book, the single number denotes the person as *he appears to be* in the eyes of his fellow beings, while the compound number represents the hidden forces in the background of the career.

In this case, the single number 3 is strong and powerful and is generally associated with ambitious people who gain positions of authority and who do especially well in government departments.

The occult symbolism of the compound number 12, is however, that of 'the Victim or the Sacrifice.'

The letters of the name MacDonald produce the single number of 5, an excellent number, as I explained before, and the compound number 32 is, as in the case of Sir Austen Chamberlain, also a good number symbolising 'the Paths of Wisdom.'

The addition, however, of the two single numbers of the name Ramsay MacDonald, 5 plus 3, produces an 8, a number which, I have explained earlier, represents two worlds, the material and the spiritual, one side associated with philosophic thought, concentration of purpose and zeal for any cause espoused and the other representing upheavals and revolutions. This combination, considered along with the meaning of the compound number that stands for his Christian name symbolises 'the Victim or the Sacrifice,' and thus foreshadowed very clearly that Ramsay MacDonald, no matter what his great qualities, would in the end be made 'the victim' or 'the sacrifice' of his political party and would face in his career upheavals and revolutions.

The addition of the numbers of the two names, that is 12 and 32 produces the compound number of 44, which in the explanation of compound numbers given in Chapter 14 reads : 'This number is full of the gravest warnings for the future. It foreshadows disasters brought about by association with others.' A decidedly ominous indication of the future of the leader of one of England's political parties. Further, as he was born on October 12th, the single number of which is a 3, is not in harmonious vibration with his Name number, an 8. Consequently one might have expected a great deal of muddle and jumble to be associated with his career.

If this man had really understood the extraordinary meaning there is in a name when transcribed into numbers, he would never have allowed his party or the public to call him by the single word Ramsay. He should never have allowed such familiarity, but should have insisted on being called, *if he could do it,* by the single word MacDonald with its magical number of 32.

Later on in this book (Chapter 32) will be found examples from the names of Presidents of the United States.

In the following chapter I will explain the symbolism that from the most ancient times has been given to what is called 'compound numbers,' and at the same time I will explain the system I have alluded to at the beginning of this chapter, whereby readers will be able to understand how it is that they can know the approach of the 'lucky day', so that they may be able to take hold of any good opportunity which may present itself.

14. THE 'COMPOUND' OR 'SPIRITUAL' NUMBERS

In the preceding chapters I have given the meanings of what are called the principal or 'single' numbers—called the 'root' numbers—from 1 to 9. I will now proceed with the next step in this curious study of Numerology, namely, the explanation of the occult symbolism given to what are called the 'double' or 'compound' numbers, and how such knowledge may be used in everyday life.

Although this is a much more advanced and more difficult part of the study of numbers, I will endeavour to make it as clear and as easy to understand as I have endeavoured to do with the single numbers in the earlier chapters. Before launching out into this side of the subject, I must, I feel, give a few words of explanation so as to prepare my readers for what is to follow.

I have already explained that the single numbers denote what the man or woman *appears to be* in the eyes of their fellow beings, while the double or compound numbers show the hidden influences that play their role behind the scenes as it were, and in some mysterious way often foreshadow the future or the hidden current of destiny of the individual.

When one passes the major or root numbers of 1 to 9, what is called the greatest symbolism of numbers commences, and continues until 5 times 9 or number 45 is reached; at this point the mystical number of 7 is brought into operation and added to the number of 45, producing 52, which stands for the 52 weeks of a year. This number of 52, multiplied by 7, gives 364 as the ordinary days of the year in that ancient period of Time when trade unionism had not made its appearance. These ancient and wonderful people, however, used the 365th day of each year as *the one great festival holiday of all, and no work of any kind* was allowed to be done by man, woman, child or beast. This number of 365 is based on the passage of the Sun through the twelve divisions of the Zodiac, which is the origin of the calculation of the year period and is found in every civilisation.

As I said before, the meaning of the single numbers from 1 to 9 represents how the man or woman appears in the eyes of his fellows. They are the numbers of *individuality and personality.*

All numbers from 10 onwards symbolise 'double' or 'compound' numbers; the number 12, if we take it for an example, has for its root or fadic number, a single number such as the 3, but at the same time the 1 and 2 of which the twelve is composed of are 'compound' and have a meaning or their own, distinct from the number 3.

How and in what age these 'compound' numbers became illustrated by symbolism, we do not know and never can know. We can only say that they appear to have always existed. Symbols may be called the Language of Nature, and as such we must take them.

The meanings ascribed to the numbers 1 to 9 belong then to *the physical or material side of things*, and 'compound' numbers from 10 onwards belong to the more *occult or spiritual side of life*. Distinct symbolism has been given to the 'compound' numbers up to that mysterious number of 52, and this symbolism I will now proceed to translate in as simple language as possible. I have already illustrated in a previous chapter by examples of the names of Lloyd George, Baldwin, Austen Chamberlain and Ramsay MacDonald, the information one is able to get by knowing the meaning of the 'compound' number and using it in relation to the information given by the single number, but later on it will be my privilege to explain a still more practical application of this knowledge which will enable one to actually pick out what days will be fortunate and what will be unfortunate, which I think will be of inestimable value to my readers.

The universally accepted symbolism of the compound numbers in ancient times was given in pictures and may still be found in the Tarot Cards which have been handed down to us from the most ancient ages and whose origin is lost in antiquity.

Ten is symbolised as the 'Wheel of Fortune.' It is a number of honour, of faith and self-confidence, of rise and fall; one's name will be known for good or evil, according to one's desires; it is a fortunate number in the sense that one's plans are likely to be successful.

Eleven is an ominous number to occultists. It gives a warning of hidden dangers, trial, and treachery from others. It has a symbol of 'a Clenched Hand,' and 'a Lion Muzzled,' and the person under the influence of this symbol will have great difficulties to contend against.

Twelve is a number which symbolises suffering and anxiety of mind. It is also indicated as 'the Sacrifice' of 'the Victim' and generally foreshadows one, being sacrificed for the plans or intrigues of others.

Thirteen is a number indicating change of plans, place, and such like, and is not unfortunate, as is generally supposed. In some of the ancient writings it is said, 'He who understands the number 13 will be given power and dominion.' It is symbolised by the picture of 'a Skeleton' or 'Death', with a scythe reaping down men, in a field of new-grown grass where young faces and heads appear cropping up on every side. It is a number of upheaval and destruction upon itself. It is a number of warning of the unknown or unexpected, if it becomes a 'compound' number in one's calculations.

Fourteen is a number of movement, combination of people and things, and danger from natural forces, such as tempests, water, air or fire. This number is fortunate for dealings with money, speculation, and changes in business, but there is always a strong element of risk and danger attached to it, which generally occurs due to the wrong actions actions and foolhardiness of others. If this number comes out in calculations of future events the person should be warned to act with caution and prudence.

Fifteen is a number of occult significance, of magic and mystery; but as a rule it does not represent the higher side of occultism, its meaning being that the persons represented by it will use every art of magic they can to carry out their purpose. If associated with a good or fortunate single number, it can be very lucky and powerful, but if associated with one of the peculiar numbers, such as a 4 or an 8, the person it represents will not hesitate to use any sort of art or even 'black magic,' to gain what he or she desires.

It is mostly associated with 'good talkers,' often possessing gifts of eloquence, Music and Art and a dramatic personality, combined with a certain voluptuous temperament and strong personal magnetism. It is a fotunate number for obtaining gifts and favours from others.

The number Sixteen has a most peculiar occult symbolism. It is symbolised by a picture of 'a Tower Struck by Lightning from which a man is falling with a Crown on his head.' It is also called 'the Shattered Citadel.'

It gives a warning of some strange fatality awaiting the person, also indicating a danger of accidents and defeat of one's plans. If it appears as a 'compound' number relating to the future, it is a warning sign that should be carefully noted and plans made in advance in an endeavour to avert its fatalistic tendency.

The number Seventeen is a highly spiritual number, and is symbolically expressed by the 8-pointed Star of Venus : a symbol of 'Peace and Love.' It is also called 'the Star of the Magi' and expresses that the person it represents has become superior in spirit to the trials and difficulties of his life or his career. It is considered as a 'number of immortality' and that the person's name 'lives after him.' It is a fortunate number if it works out in relation to future events, provided it is not associated with the single numbers of fours and eights.

Eighteen is a number which has a difficult symbolism to translate. It is (Symbolised by a picture of) 'a rayed moon from which drops of blood are falling; a wolf and a hungry dog are seen below catching the falling drops of blood in their opened mouths, while still lower a crab is seen hastening to join them.' It is symbolic of materialism striving to destroy the spiritual side of the nature. It generally associates a person with bitter quarrels, even quarrels within the family, also with war, social upheavals, revolutions; and in some cases it indicates making money and position through wars or by wars. It is, however, a warning against treachery, deception by others, and also indicates danger from elements, such as storm, water, fires, and explosions. When this 'compound' number appears in working out dates in advance, such a date should be selected with a great amount of care, caution, and circumspection.

The number Nineteen is regarded as fortunate and extremely favourable. It is symbolised as 'the Sun' and is called 'the Prince of Heaven.' It is a number which promises of happiness, success, esteem, and honour, and also success in one's plans for the future.

Twenty is a number which is called 'the Awakening,' and also 'the Judgement.' It is symbolised by the figure of a winged angel sounding a trumpet, while from below a man, a woman, and a child are seen rising from a tomb with their hands clasped in prayer.

This number has a peculiar interpretation : the awakening of new purpose, new plans, new ambitions, the call to action, but for some great purpose, cause or duty. It is not a material number and consequently wordly success cannot be assured.

If used in relation to a future event, it denotes delays, hindrances to one's plans, which can only be conquered through the development of the spiritual side of the nature.

The number Twenty one is symbolised by the picture of 'the Universe, and it is also called 'the Crown of the Magi.' It is a number of advancement, honours, elevation in life, and general success. It means victory after a long fight for 'the Crown of the Magi' is only gained after long initiation and tests of determination. It is a fortunate number promising success if it appears in any connection regarding future events.

The number Twenty two is symbolised by 'a Good Man blinded by the folly of others, with a knapsack on his back full of Errors.' In this picture he appears to offer no defence against a ferocious tiger which is attacking him. It is a number which warns of illusion and delusion, representing a good person who lives in a fool's paradise; a dreamer of dreams who awakens only when surrounded by danger. It is also a number of false judgement owing to the influence of others.

As a number in connection with future events its warning and meaning should be carefully noted.

The number Twenty three is called 'the Royal Star of the Lion.' It is a number which promise of success, help from superiors and protection from those in high places. In dealing with future events it is a most fortunate number and a promise of success for one's plans.

The number Twenty four is also fortunate; it promises the assistance and association of those in rank and position with one's plans; it also denotes gain through love of the opposite sex; it is a favourable number when it comes out in relation to future events.

Twenty five is a number denoting strength gained through experience, and benefits obtained through observation of people and things. It is not deemed exactly 'lucky' as its success is achieved after strife and trials in the earlier life. It is favourable when it appears in regard to the future.

Twenty six is a number full of the gravest warnings for the future. It foreshadows disasters brought about by association with others; ruin, by bad speculations, by partnerships, unions, and bad advice.

If it comes out in connection with future events one should carefully consider the path one is treading into.

Twenty seven is a good number and is symbolised as the Sceptre. It is promises authority, power and command. It indicates that reward will come from the productive intellect; that the creative faculties have sown good seeds that will reap a harvest. Persons with this 'compound' number at their back should carry out their own ideas and plans. It is a fortunate number if it appears in any connection with future events.

The number Twenty eight is full of contradictions. It indicates that a person of great promise and possibilities is likely to see all taken away from him unless he carefully provides for the future. It indicates loss through trust in others, opposition and competition in trade, danger of loss through law, and the likelihood of having to begin (life's journey from scratch a number of times). It is not a fortunate number in relation to future events.

The number Twenty nine indicates uncertainties, treacheries, and deception from others; it foreshadows trials, tribulation, and unexpected dangers, unreliable friends, and grief and deception caused by members of the opposite sex. It gives grave warning if it comes out in anything concerning future events.

Thirty is a number of thoughtful deduction, retrospection and mental superiority over one's fellows, but, as it seems to belong completely to the mental plane, the persons it represents are likely to put all material things on one side—not because they have to, but because they wish to do so. For this reason it is neither fortunate, nor unfortunate for either depends on the mental outlook of the person it represents. It can be all powerful, but it is just as often indifferent according to the will or desire of the person.

Thirty one is a number very similar to the preceding one, except that the person it represents is even more self-contained, lonely, and isolated from his fellow beings. It is not a fortunate number from a worldly or material standpoint.

The number Thirty two has a magical power like the single 5 or the 'compound' numbers 14 and 23. It is usually associated with combinations of people or nations. It is a fortunate number if the person it represents holds to his own judgement and opinions; if not, his plans are likely to become wrecked by the stubbornness and stupidity of others. It is a favourable number if it appears in connection with future events.

The number Thirty three has no potency of its own, and consequently has the same meaning as the number 24 which is also a 6 and next to it in its own series of 'compound' numbers.

Thirty four has the same meaning as the number 25, which is next to it in its own series of 'compound' numbers.

Thirty five has the same meaning as the number 26, which is next to it in its own series of compound numbers.

Thirty six has the same meaning as the number 27, which is next to it in its own series of 'compound' numbers.

The number Thirty seven has a distinct potency of its own. It is a number predicting of good and fortunate association in love, and in relations concerning the opposite sex. It is also good for partnership of all kinds. It is a fortunate indication if it appears in connection with future events.

Thirty eight has the same meaning as the number 29, which is next to it in its own series of 'compound' numbers.

Thirty nine has the same meaning as the number 30, which is next to it in its own series of 'compound' numbers.

Forty has the same meaning as the number 31, which is next to it in its own series of 'compound' numbers.

Forty one has the same meaning as the number 32, which is the next to it in its own series of 'compound' numbers.

Forty two has the same meaning as the number 24.

Forty three is an unfortunate number. It is symbolised by the signs of revolution, upheaval, strife, failure, and prevention, and is not a fortunate number if it comes out in calculation relating to future events.

Forty four has the same meaning as 26.
Forty five has the same meaning as 27.
Forty six has the same meaning as 37.
Forty seven has the same meaning as 29.
Forty eight has the same meaning as 30.
Forty nine has the same meaning as 31.
Fifty has the same meaning as 32.

The number Fifty one has a very powerful potency of its own. It represents the nature of the warrior; it promises sudden advancement in whatever one undertakes; it is especially favourable for those in military or naval life and for leaders in any cause. At the same time it threatens of encountering enemies, danger, and the likelihood of assassination.

Fiftytwo has the same meaning as 43.

We have now completed the 52 numbers which represent the 52 weeks of one year, and for all practical purposes there is no necessity to proceed farther. I will now show my readers the method of employing the symbolism of these 'compound' numbers, together with the 'single' numbers whose meaning they have learned earlier in this book.

The rule to follow is : One must add the date one wishes to know about to the total of the compound numbers of ones name, see what number this gives and read the meaning I have given to the added number.

Example : I will suppose you wish to know if, say Monday the 26th April will be a favourable day for you to carry out some plan: let us say, to ask for a rise in your position or in your wages. Take the number given to each letter of your name from the alphabet I have shown you, add to the total 'compound' number or its single digit the number given by the addition of the 26th April, 2 plus 6 and 8, add this 8 to the total of your Name number and Birth number and look up the meaning I have given to the final number produced, and you will find at once whether Monday, the 26th, will be favourable to you or not. If you see that it does not give a fortunate number, then add the next day, the 27th or the next until you come to a date that is indicated as favourable. Act on the favourable date thus shown, and you will find that the day thus indicated will be fortunate for you.

Suppose that you are John Smith born on 8th January, work the name out as follows:

J	=	1	S	=	3
O	=	7	M	=	4
H	=	5	I	=	1
N	=	5	T	=	4
		18 = 9	H	=	5
					17 = 8

You now add the 9 and the 8 together, which gives you the 'compound' number of 17, whose units added together gives 8. To this add the 8 produced by similar means from the 26th April this gives you the number 16, with 7 for the single number; now add the Birth number 8th January to this 7 and you obtain 15 for the last compound number with 6 for the last single number.

Look up the meaning I have given to the compound Number 15: you will find it stated for obtaining money, gifts, and favours from others, it is a fortunate number. Therefore the occult influences playing on John Smith, born 8th January, would be favourable on the 26th April for his using that date to ask favours or carrying out his plans. If it had not given favourable indications John Smith should then work out the 27th April or the next day or the next, until he found a date indicated as fortunate.

The same rule applies for every name and every date of birth.

15. HOW TO USE 'SINGLE' AND 'COMPOUND' NUMBERS

Following the publication of some articles I published in a leading London paper, I received some thousands of letters asking for further information as to how to make the Birth number and the Name number accord, I have, therefore, worked out the following example.

If possible, make the Birth number and the number given by the Name agree; the vibration will then all be in harmony, and will give a greater promise of success if the number is a favourable one.

As an illustration, take again the example I gave in the previous chapter, of John Smith :

J	=	1	S	=	3
O	=	7	M	=	4
H	=	5	I	=	1
N	=	5	T	=	4
			H	=	5

18=1 Plus 8 = 9   17 = 1 plus 7 = 8

The single number of John totals to 9, and the single number of Smith equals to 8; the 8 and 9 added together make 17, and 1 plus 7 makes 8. The number of the entire Name is therefore an 8. If John Smith were born on any day making an 8, such as the 8th, 17th or 26th of a month, the number of the Name and the number of the Birth *would then be in harmony,* and although the 8 is not such a lucky number to have in an ordinary way, yet in such a case there would be no clash in the *numbers;* and if John Smith, knowing this, used the dates making an 8, such as the 8th, 17th or 26th, for his important transactions, he would find himself more fortunate.

If, on the contrary, he had another number, say 2, as his Birth number, such as the 2nd, 11th, 20th or 29th, his Name and his Birth number would *not be in vibration one to the other,* and there would always be a muddle or jumble in his affairs, and he would also be unable to decide which number to act on or what date he should use.

As he cannot alter his Birth number, then the thing to do is to alter the *Name number.* If he added a letter making a 3 to his name, such as a C, a G, an L or an S, which as I have mentioned in an earlier chapter have the number 3, and wrote his name, as 'John C. Smith' or 'John G. Smith', and insisted on being known and called as that, this new Number 3, added to the 17, which John Smith made before, would now give a total of 20 or a single number of 2, and then both the Name number and the Birth number *would be in harmonious vibration together,* and he would also be sure that he would be right in selecting any date that makes a 2, such as the 2nd, 11th, 20th or 29th of any month, as the most favourable day to make any change or carry out any important plan.

If however 'John Smith' was born under an 8, such as the 8th, 17th or 26th of any month, as the total of the numbers of his name also make an 8, I would then not advise him to add a letter or change the Name number, but to work under the 8, as I explained earlier.

Surely, this is a simple, and clear rule, and will help those countless readers who may be puzzled as to how to get their Name number and Birth number to accord.

However, if a person is born under either of those peculiar numbers such as a 4 or an 8, and if the Name number should also total up to a 4 when one is born under an 8 or to an 8 when one is born under a 4, then for material success it would be better if one added some letter, as I explained in the case of John Smith, so that the total of your number is no longer a 4 or an 8, but one with a more fortunate vibration, making, say, a 1, 3, 6 or 9. Such a change in the majority of cases will produce more fortunate results and set up entirely new vibrations, which will change a lonely, unlucky life into one of happiness and success.

I would also strongly advise all those who have the combination of 4 and 8 when they make the change by altering their name to produce another number, such as a 1,3,6 or 9, to wear the colours and jewels I have set out for these numbers in an earlier chapter in this book dealing with 'single' numbers, and I am absolutely confident that they will never regret having followed my advice.

I also advise that in order to get the best advantage out of one's numbers, while living in cities and towns a person should select an accomodation whose number also gives the same vibration as the Birth and Name number. If they live in the country they should give a name to their house which produce the same number as the Birth and the Name number. Especially in the case of a person having an 8 for the Birth number and a 4 for the Name number or vice versa, they should, under no circumstances, live in a house whose number worked out to the single digit of a 4 or an 8.

16. WHY THE BIRTH NUMBER IS THE MOST IMPORTANT

The Birth number is the easiest and simplest to use for everyday matters, especially for all those who are not advanced students in occult symbolism. It indicates with authority and precision the exact date for action, namely a date which will be *in accord and harmony with the Birth number*, and the rules concerning it are simple and easy to understand.

A person born on, say, the 1st, 10th, 19th or 28th, of any month will be quite safe in picking out any one of these dates as the best date for any important action. As the number 4 is what may be called the feminine or negative side of the 1, he or she can take this number as *an associate number*, but on account of the peculiar qualities of this number 1, I do not advise it to be chosen for any *worldly or material affairs*. This number 4 will on several occassions come into the lines of number 1 people, *on its own* and it will mostly prove to be a fatal number which will have an influence on their lives *outside of their control* and it certainly is not connected with the happier side of life. In many instances of number 1 people in my knowledge, the number 4, such as the 4th, 13th, 22nd, and 31st, has brought on these dates the news of an accident, a death or a sorrow which has played some important part in their lives. The number 1 people also often find that they seem unconsciously drawn to live in houses whose number makes a 4, such as a house in a terrace or street numbered 4, 13, 22, 31, 40, 49, etc., and although such houses may be proved to be associated with important events in the career, yet I have seldom found them associated with happy *material* advantages.

A person whose Birth number is an 8 should certainly never live in a house whose number makes a 4, 13, 22, 31, 40, etc., and neither should a person whose Birth number makes a 4 live in a house whose number makes an 8, 17, 26, 35, 44, etc., not, at least, if they wish to escape sorrow, misfortune, and strange fatality.

The second best numbers for a person whose Birth number makes a 1 are the interchangeable numbers of 2 and 7, and dates these numbers make, such as the 2nd, 7th, 11th, 16th, 20th, 25th or 29th, and houses under the numbers 2,7,11, 16, 20,25,29,34, etc., are generally not unfavourable; but as these numbers are related to change or unsettled conditions, the number 1 person seldom settles down in houses under the numbers 2 and 7, or find conditions brought into his or her life under the dates given by these numbers as relating to *fixed or settled matters*.

Under the law of harmony and vibration there is no question but that number 1 person should be associated as much as possible with the same number 2 in all its forms. Persons born under the 3 should employ their number 3, and so on for all the numbers with the exception of those born under the 4 and the 8. In the latter cases I recommend, then, *not to increase* the peculiar influence of the 4 and 8, but to choose more fortunate vibrations.

This is where the power and knowledge of the Name number will apply. A number 4 or a number 8 person who desires to get under more fortunate vibration, as they cannot alter their Birth number they can at least *change their Name number* and live under it and so become equally as fortunate as those whose Birth number is a lucky one.

I will give an example of what I mean.

Suppose a man or woman has been born on, say, the 8th, 17th or 26th of January, and the Name number works out, let us say, to a final total of a 1,3, 5 or 6 (I have purposely taken the strong or positive numbers). Then I most certainly advise the number 8 persons to drop using the 8 in all their transactions and use instead any strong number the name may give, such as a 1, 3, 5 or 6, and a number 4 person should do likewise.

You will notice I have not used the 9 in giving this rule, and my reason for not doing so is that the 4 which is the symbol of the planet Uranus, and the 8, which represents the planet Saturn, are so antagonistic in their qualities to the 9, the symbol of Mars, that it is better to keep such numbers apart.

This may sound strange to those who have not made any study of occultism, but believe me, the above rule is not laid down at random or by any shadowy guess-work; on the contrary, it has a solid foundation in the science of the planet, and anyone who has ever studied Astrology will tell you that I am right when I say that any combination of the planets of Mars (9) and Saturn (8) or Uranus (4) can only foreshadow troubles and disasters of all kinds.

To resume, the reason I advise that the Birth number is the most important as the Key to the main 'fadic' number influencing the life is that in the first place it is unalterable; secondly, it is related to the planet's influence at the moment of birth, and thirdly, by some mysterious law of vibration—which, even if we do not understand, we must admit to existense even in such so-called inanimate objects as crystals, molecules, and atoms. The moment of birth decides the note of harmony or vibration, and so has its influence on the actions of our lives from the cradle to the grave.

Further, the Birth number relates to the material side of life, the Name number to the more occult or spiritual side of our existence.

Also the Name number is more difficult to be sure of —*it must be the product of the name we are most known by.* This presents a problem for the average man or woman. Many men are more known by their surnames than by their Christian and surname together, and many women are called by some 'pet' name to the complete extinction of their Christian name. In working out such cases mistakes may easily be made and a number may be allotted which is not the correct one, whereas by going by the Birth number and using it as the foundation no mistake can be made. If, then, it is found that the name one thinks is the correct one, and if its number gives the same number or any degree of the same number as the Birth number, then one can be absolutely certain that no mistake is being made, for if both the Name number and the Birth number are in accordance there is nothing one can desire better.

If the Name number does not accord with the Birth number, it can be made agreeable by the addition of an initial or an alteration in the Christian name, so that both give the same vibration; and I advise this to be done in every case where the Birth and Name numbers do not agree, except in the case of the numbers 4 and 8 of which I have made a mention, in the beginning of the chapter.

Those who are advanced students in occult symbolism can utilise the hidden meaning given by both Christian and surnames to work out the finer shades of destiny, but for all ordinary cases—and I must not lose sight of the fact that I am writing this book for the average man and woman, those who want to help themselves in the easiest possible way, and who have, perhaps, no time for deep and abstruse study—to all those, I know I cannot do better than to advise them to follow closely the rules governing the Birth number as set out in these pages.

Note : The numbers like the month of Birth or the year of Birth is not *so personal or so intimate* in regard to close calculations as is the number of the day of Birth.

The number of the month is useful regarding general matters, and the number of the year to the wider current of events.

Example : If a person is born, on 6th June, 1866, then the numbers of his birth day, birth month and birth year can be written down in the following order :

6th	= 6 (Individual or Personal)
June	= 5 (General Matters)
1866 = 21	= 3 (Current of Destiny)

The number 6, 5, and 3 should be regarded as separate and distinct and should not be added together.

The year number totalled and added to itself indicates an important year in the Destiny.

Example :   1866 = 21
                 21

                1887

A further illustration of this is given in a later chapter where the case of William I of Prussia is presented.

17. SOME ILLUSTRATIONS OF NAME AND NUMBERS

As it is impossible in a book of this size to go into every shade of the occult significance of numbers that spring from the foundation of 1 to 9, I must confine myself to giving a few illustrations of how to use the numbers allotted to the letters of the Hebrew alphabet for the purpose of showing how Destiny appears interwoven with numbers and names.

The great Napoleon originally wrote his name as Napoleon Buonaparte. Later on in his life he changed it to Napoleon Bonaparte. This change had a curious significance :

        Napoleon equals to number 5
        Buonaparte equals to number 5

The number 5, as I showed earlier in these pages, is considered a magical number and was carried by the ancient Greeks as a mascot when they went into battle. The two numbers of 5, if added, producing 10, are equally important and strangely significant in this case.

When Napoleon altered the spelling to Bonaparte, it altered the vibration of this word to an 8, and if you refer to what I said about this number you will find on the lower plane it represents revolution, anarchy, waywardness, conflict with human justice, and on a lower plane futher, a tragic ending to the life. Although a great man, Napoleon was on the lower plane of existence, as can be seen if one looks up how the number 8 (Saturn) and the 9 (Mars) dominated the chief events of his career. As Napoleon Bonaparte, the two names add up to form number 13, which, in the occult symbolism that accompanies this system of letters and numbers, bears the curious picture of a skeleton with a scythe *mowing men down*, also a symbol of 'Power' which 'if wrongly used will bring destruction upon itself.'

This was so borne out by Napoleon's career that further comment is unnecessary.

Some remarkable illustration of the significance of names and numbers may be had from the examples of ships.

The United States battleship *Maine*, which exploded mysteriously in the Havana Harbour, killing every man on board has its compound number 16 which as you must have read earlier symbolises, 'A Tower Struck by Lighting.' The mystery of the blowing up of this warship has never been solved, but it caused the declaration of war by the United States against Spain.

Another tragic ship disaster was that of the *Waratah* which, after leaving Australia, sank with all her passengers and crew as if she had been swallowed up by the ocean. The number of the word 'Waratah' equals 20, which, as you have read in Chapter 14, is called 'the judgement'. This number is symbolised by the figure of a winged angel sounding a trumpet, while from below a man, a woman, and a child are seen rising from a tomb with their hands clasped in prayer.

Yet another illustration might be taken from the fate of the *Leinster*, the Holyhead and Kingstown mail-boat that was torpedoed by a German submarine within sight of the Irish coast during the last months of the 1914-1918 War.

The word 'Leinster' gives the compound number of 28, 'a number full of contradictions' which also indicates 'loss through trust in others.' This boat was carrying a large number of soldiers as well as passengers, who certainly trusted their lives to others, in the belief that the boat would be accompanied by some of the destroyers from Kingtown Harbour. For some unexplained reason the order to the destroyers never came—the *Leinster* sailed alone, and in less than an hour met her fate and lost several hundred lives.

I know two men who decided at the last moment not to travel by that boat on that particular night because they noticed that the compound number of their name, that is 28, was the same as that of *Leinster*, and as they had read that in this system of symbolism it is not a fortunate number, and being struck by the coincidence of the name of the boat making the same number, both men took their luggage off at the last moment, and so escaped.

It is quite natural that under the tension of war, people are more inclined to watch for the slightest clue that might give a warning of danger. I know of many instances where men actually saved their lives by following the clue given by this system of numbers. In one case a man resting by the side of his battery was amusing himself asking the birth dates of the men around him. He was startled to find that they were all born under the number 8, he himself being born on the 26th January, a number 8 man in the 'period of the 8.' It was precisely then that it dawned upon him that the day was also an 8, namely 17th February, and looking up, he counted the number of the battery, *it was also on 8.* Just then a German gun opened fire. He counted the shells as they dropped, each one coming nearer and nearer. As the seventh fell he could not resist the dread that overcame him—he rushed out into the open, and as he did so, the eighth shell struck his battery—he was the only one who escaped.

18. HOW NUMBERS RECUR IN LIVES

Among my collection on the influence of numbers in connection with events, I have many that are decidedly interesting.

The following appeared in many of the London newspapers:

Sir Alma-Tadema, the famous artist, says his important number is 17. He was 17 when he first met his wife; their first house had the same number; it was on August 17th that the work of rebuilding his home began, and it was on November 17th that he took up his residence there. His second marriage was in 1871, which when added together gives the number 17. His house, in the artistic quarter of St. John's Wood, was again a multiple of 17. Sir Alma-Tadema was born on January 8th, which if separated to form a double digited date will give 17, a date having such a great importance in his life.

King Edward VII was born on the 9th of November in a month that is called in Astrology 'the second house of Mars' and governed by 9, the number of Mars. His marriage took place in the year 1863, which if added together gives the number 9; his coronation was to take place on the 27th of June, which adds upto make a 9, and he was actually crowned on August 9th.

King Edward often referred to me 'as the man who would not let him live past 69'. On the occasion when I first had the honour of meeting him as Prince of Wales in Lady Arthur Paget's house, he asked me to 'work out his numbers.' I did so and explained the reason how his 'fadic' or root numbers were the 6 and the 9. I then told him that the coming together of these two numbers would be his fatal year, and further that the event would take place on a day making the number 6 and in a month governed by the 6, which would be May. He never forgot my prediction, and it is my melancholic privilege to record that the last occasion when I had any conversation with his late Majesty was a few weeks before his death. He was joining the royal train at Victoria to make his usual journey to the Continent when he noticed me, as I too was going abroad. He sent an equerry to call me, and he said, smiling broadly—"Well, Cheiro, I'm still alive, as you see, but from that warning of yours, as I am now in my 69th year, I must take care." He then spoke briefly of his racing wagers, and concluded by emphasising how remarkably my advice had been crowned by success.

Alas, in a few short weeks he returned to Buckingham Palace, and the public heard with consternation of his illness, which proved fatal. On May 6th, in his 69th year, the first time when these 'fadic' numbers came together—my prediction was fulfilled.

Incidentally, King Edward mentioned that his 'dear friend' as he called him, Lord Randolph Churchill, was extremely superstitious with regard to the number 13, and attributed many adverse events to the fact that he was born on the 13th of February, 1849. 1849 when added together formed the number 22, which when again added formed a 4.

I explained to King Edward that the idea that 13 is an unfortunate number was not supported by occultism; that it was in fact an important number if persons were born on the 4th, 13th, 22nd or 31st, and it was simply regarded as ill-omened because in occultism it was looked upon with veneration.

A few years before his death in London in January, 1895, I had a brief interview with this famous statesman, and he reminded me that my theory of numbers had interested him very much. From King Edward he had gathered that I thought 4 to be his fadic number, and I confirmed this. It was also represented in almost all the leading events of his life.

Another remarkable instance of prediction by numbers was in the case of my meeting with Sir Charles Russell. I explained to him that his important numbers were the 1 and the 4, with what are called their interchangeable numbers of 2 and 7, and that he would reach the highest position that his career could give him on a date that made a 1, such as the 1st, 10th, 19th or 28th; in a month governed by the 2 and 7, such as July, which is governed by those numbers, and in a year whose number added up to give the number 4. He made a careful note of this, and when he wore his robes of Lord Chief Justice of England for the first time he invited me to the Law Courts. After the ceremony of installation he came to me in his private room and as a souvenir gave me a signed impression of his hand.

19. UNFOUNDED DREAD OF THE NUMBER '13'

Nearly all people have an extraordinary dread of the number 13, which, if they only knew the real truth, is not at all the unlucky number they imagine it to be.

The origin of this dread is due primarily to the fact that it was much used in connection with occultism, and was in far-off times regarded as a powerful although a fatal number. As I have stated before in the previous pages, in some of the old writing of famous Adepts it is said, 'He who understands the number 13 hath the keys of power and dominion.'

The opposition of the early Church to occultism was one of the principal reasons why this number became a 'taboo.' It was given out that as 13 sat down to the Last Supper it would be unlucky if 13 were to eat together, and that one of the 13 would die within the year, and so forth.

I must say I could never see the logic of this, for if Christ had not been crucified the Scriptures would not have been written, in which case Christianity would never have existed.

There was another reason, however, why 13 was dreaded, and this was because the occult symbolism that stood for this number was represented by a mystic picture of 'a skeleton with a scythe in its bony hands reaping down men.' It was a curious picture that few could understand, and those who did kept their knowledge to themselves in an age when even to speak of such things was to forfeit ones life by torture or at stake.

The picture allotted to the number 13, although drawn or painted in many different ways, always contained the same idea—a skeleton reaping in a field, hands and feet springing up among new-grown grass, the crowned head of a man fallen at the point of the scythe, while a female head with flowing hair parted in the centre appeared in the background. To find the true interpretation of this weird picture one must go back to the meaning attached to the single number 4, of which the 13 makes a second 4 in its compound number.

The single 4, as you have read earlier, is a strange number in itself. Persons dominated by it are usually misunderstood and lonely in their lives; they would bring about opposition and secret enemies would be constantly at work against them; they reverse the order of things in communities and governments; they are attracted to social questions and reforms of all kinds; they rebel against authority and set up new dynasties or republic.

The number 13 has all these qualities in its higher scale, but even more accentuated. It cuts down all before it, reversing the order of things shown by the hands and feet springing up in the grass and the crowned head falling before the scythe. The female head in the background denotes social reform, the new order of things, and the uplifting of woman, and so forth.

It was perhaps this picture of a skeleton with a scythe in its bony fingers, calling up the idea of Death in the minds of those who could not understand the inner meaning of the symbolism, that made the number 13 to be so dreaded.

If people will, however, only think, they will see that 13 belongs to the series of 4, in the range of 4, 13, 22, 31, etc., and consequently a person born, say on the 4th, 13th, 22nd or 31st of a month will find all these numbers recurring in their careers, and this being so, 13 will crop up just as often as the other numbers which make a 4.

In many hotels, even the modern ones, there is no Room 13; and a similar peculiarity characterises the seats of opera-houses in Italy.

But the dread of 13 has only a limited geographical range.

In the East and in the West the number is honoured. In the Indian Pantheon there are 13 Buddhas. The mystical discs which surmount Indian and Chinese pagodas are 13 in number. Enshrined in the Temple of Atsusa, in Japan, is a sacred sword with 13 objects of mystery forming its hilt. Turning Westward, 13 was the sacred number of the Mexicans, they had 13 snake gods.

The original States that formed the Amercian Union were 13; its motto, *E Pluribus Unum*, has 13 letters, the American eagle has 13 feather in each wing, and when George Washington raised the Republican standard he was saluted with 13 guns.

20. THE SIMILARITY OF NUMBERS IN THE LIVES OF ST. LOUIS AND LOUIS XVI

One of the most remarkable instances I have ever come across of numbers pointing to a sequence of similar events in lives as far apart as over five hundred years, and which might be used as evidence of reincarnation, is the extraordinary case of St. Louis of France and King Louis XVI, which was published in 1852 in a book called *Research into the Efficacy of Dates and Names in the Annals of Nations.*

As history shows, there was an interval of exactly 539 years between the birth of St. Louis and Louis XVI.

If one adds this interval number to the remarkable dates in the life of St. Louis, a parallel of events, even to similarity in names, will be seen in the events in the life of Louis XVI.

ST. LOUIS		LOUIS XVI	
Birth of St. Louis 23rd April	1215	Birth of Louis XVI 23rd August,	
Add interval	539		
	1754		1754
Birth of Isabel, sister of St. Louis	1225	Birth of Elizabeth, sister of Louis XVI	
Add interval	539		
	1764		1764
Death of Louis VIII, father of St.Louis	1226	Death of the Dauphin, father of Louis XVI	
Add interval	539		
	1765		1765
Minority of St. Louis Commences	1226	Minority of Louis XVI commences	
Add interval	539		
	1765		1765
Marriage of St.Louis	1231	Marriage of Louis XVI	
Add interval	539		
	1770		1770

Majority of St.Louis (King) King	1235	Accession of Louis XVI, of France
Add interval	<u>539</u>	
	1774	1774
St.Louis concludes a peace treaty with Henry III	1243	Louis XVI concludes a peace treaty with George III
Add interval	<u>539</u>	
	1782	1782
An Eastern prince ends an Ambassador to St.Louis desiring to become a Christian	1249	An Eastern Prince sends an ambassador to Louis XVI for the same purpose
Add interval	<u>539</u>	
	1788	1788
Captivity of St.Louis	1250	Louis XVI deprived of all power
Add interval	<u>539</u>	
	1789	1789
St.Louis abandoned	1250	Louis XVI abandoned
Add interval	<u>539</u>	
	1789	1789
Birth of Tristian(Sorrow)	1250	Fall of the Bastille and Commencement of the Revolution
Add interval	<u>539</u>	
	1789	1789
Beginning of Pastoral under Jacob	1250	Beginning of the Jacobins in France
Add interval	<u>539</u>	
	1789	1789
Death of Isabel d' Angoulême		Birth of Isabel d' Angoulême in France
	1250	
Add interval	<u>539</u>	
	1789	1789
Death of Queen Blanche, mother of St.Louis	1253	End of the White Lily of France
Add interval	<u>539</u>	
	1792	1792

St. Louis desires to retire and become a Jacobin		Louis XVI quits life at the hands of the Jacobins	
	1254		
Add interval	539		
	1793		1793
St.Louis returns to Madeleine en Provence	1254	Louis XVI entered the cemetery of the Madeleine in Paris	
Add interval	539		
	1793		1793

This, I believe, is one of the most curious examples of history repeating itself at a fixed interval. The addition of the interval number 539 reduced to the single digit gives the number 8, and the number of letters in the name Louis XVI also gives the number 8. This number, as I explained earlier, represents the symbol of Justice and of one appealing from the brutality of Human Justice to that of the Divine.

21. PERIODICITY IN NUMBERS

The Law of Periodicity can be seen in some lives in a very remarkable manner. In many cases it may last for hundreds of years, as may be noticed in the lives of St. Louis and Louis XVI in the interval of 539 years that separated these two Kings of France, and which interval when added to the date of the important events in St. Louis life, repeated similar events in the career of Louis XVI. This is considered as one of the most curious examples in history.

Further, it will be noticed that St. Louis was born on April 23rd, the numbers added together producing a 5. Louis XVI was born on August 23rd, also producing a 5.

These names worked out by the Hebrew Alphabet forms;

```
S A I N T              L O U I S
3 1 1 5 4              3 7 6 1 3
 14 = 5                 20 = 2

         5 and 2 = 7

L O U I S              X V I
3 7 6 1 3               1 6
 20 = 2                  7
                    2 and 7 = 9
```

The name Saint Louis worked out to its single digit gives 7, the spiritual number. Louis XVI worked out to its single digit gives 9, the material number. These two single numbers added together give 16 for the compound number, the occult meaning being, as you have read in a previous chapter, 'A Tower Struck by Lightning from which a man is falling with a Crown on his head', a fitting symbol in every sense for the downfall of Louis XVI.

After this date, the execution of Louis XVI, in 1793, we cannot yet trace this curious law of periodicity farther, but in adding the interval number again to 1793 we get the year 2332, in which perhaps another incarnation of St. Louis will again reign in France.

The following is another interesting example of a number being associated with the Kings of France :

The first King of France named Henri was consecrated on *14th* May, 1029, and the last King of the name of Henri was assassinated on *14th* May, 1610.

Fourteen letters it will be found make the name of Henri de Bourbon, who was the *14th* King to bear the title of King of France and Navarre.

On *14th* December, 1553 or 14 centuries, 14 decades, and 14 years after the birth of Christ, Henri IV of France was born; the figures of the date 1553 added together also make the number 14.

On *14th* May, 1554, Henri II signed the decree for the enlargement of the Rule de la Ferronnerie. The cause of this order was the narrowness of this street. The non-execution of this order resulted in the assassination of Henri IV *in that same street exactly 14 years later.*

On *14th* May, 1552, Marquerite de Valois, the first wife of Henri IV, was born.

On *14th* May 1588, the Duke of Guise opened the revolt against Henri III.

On *14th* March, 1590, Henri IV won the important Battle of Ivry.

On *14th* May, 1590, the main Army of Henri IV was defeated at the Fauxbourg of Paris.

On *14th* November, 1590, 'the Sixteen' took an oath of death rather than serve Henri IV.

On *14th* November, 1592 the French Parliament accepted the Papal Bull, which gave authority to the legate of Rome to nominate a king instead of Henri IV.

On *14th* December 1599, the Duke of Savoy submitted to Henri IV.

On *14th* September, the Dauphin, who later became Louis XIII, was baptised.

On *14th* May, 1610, owing to the narrowness of the Rue de la Feronnerie (the street his father Henri II had planned to enlarge), the carriage of King Henri IV was stopped by a cart which gave Ravaillac the opportunity to assassinate him.

On *14th* May, 1643, Louis XIII, the son of Henri IV died, on the same day of the same month that his father was killed, and if the figures of 1643 are added together they make the Number 14, which had played such an important part in his father's career.

Louis XIV ascended the throne in 1643, which also forms a *14, and died in 1715, which also make a 14.* His age at his death was 77, again making a 14.

Louis XV ascended the throne in 1715 which also equals to 14.

Louis XVI was in the *14th* year of his reign when he convoked the States-General, which brought about the Revolution and his downfall.

The Restoration of the Bourbons took place in 1814, the number of this year added together *makes* 14.

The reason why this number 14 or its single number 5 appears so much associated with the destiny of France may be traced to the fact that in Astrology Paris has always been represented as governed by the Sign Virgo, whose Planet is Mercury in its negative aspect, whose number is a 5.

During the period of French history I have cited, Paris was the principal point of power. The king who reigned in Paris ruled in France. The addition of important dates often appears to bring out subsequent dates of equal importance.

The following is a striking illustration from French history:

Revolution in France and fall of Robespierre
 took place in 1794
The numbers of this date added together give 21

The fall of Napoleon 1815
 1815 added gives 15

Fall of Charles X and Revolution in France 1830
 1830 added gives 12

Death of the king Louis Philippe 1842
 1842 added gives 15

End of Crimean War 1857
 1857 added gives 21

The famous Treaty of Berlin 1878
    1878 added gives 24
Danger of War with England over Fashoda 1902
    1902 added gives 12

World War I 1914
    1914 added gives 15
Another year of crisis in
    The French history 1929

Another curious example of the addition of dates, much commented on in both Berlin and Paris during 1914, is as follows:

In 1849, William I of Prussia fled with his mother, Queen Louis, and took refuge in England. On meeting a woman well versed in Numerology, he asked her to tell him his future. "Add, she answered, the figures of this important year together."

$$\begin{array}{r} 1849 \\ \underline{22} \\ 1871 \end{array}$$

"In the year produced by this addition you will end a great war and will be proclaimed Emperor."

"And then—?" asked the King.

"Add 1871," she replied, "and you will get the year of your death." The king made the addition and wrote 1888.

"And what of my country after that?" the king asked.

"Add again," she answered, "and see what the total is".

The king added $\begin{array}{r} 1888 \\ \underline{25} \\ 1913 \end{array}$

"In that year," the woman said, "the man who wears your crown will prepare another war, which will bring about his ruin and that of your country, for the time being."

This story was repeated to me by a close relative of the ex-Kaiser when he visited me in Paris in 1904.

In Rome there is a very ancient tradition which says that no Pope who occupies the Chair of St. Peter can reign longer than 25 years. The Popes who came very near this strangely set period were the following:

Pius VI who reigned 24 years 6 months and 14 days
Adrian I who reigned 23 years 10 months and 17 days
Pius VII who reigned 23 years 5 months and 6 days
Alexander III who reigned 21 years 11 months and 23 days
Sylvester I who reigned 21 years 0 months and 4 days

Leo XIII entered his 25th year as Pope, but did not continue beyond the set period, although he occupied the Chair of St. Peter longer than any of his predecessors.

English history also contains many equally strange examples of numbers and dates reappearing continually in remarkable lives.

On 29th May, 1630,	Charles II was born.
On 29th, May, 1660,	he was restored to the Throne.
On 29th, May, 1672,	his fleet was destroyed by the Dutch.
On 29th, May, 1679,	the Covenanter Rebellion broke out.
On 3rd, September,	Cromwell was born.
On 3rd, September,	he won the Battle of Dunbar.
On 3rd, September,	he won the Battle of Worcester.
On 3rd, September,	he died.

In a previous chapter, I have related the curious influence the numbers 6 and 9 had in the life of King Edward VII.

22. THE PHILOSOPHY OF NUMBERS

The two schools of philosophy in regard to the subject of numbers are the Pythagorean and the more ancient one known as the Chaldean.

The Greek Philosopher, Pythagoras, imbibed all his knowledge of the occult value of numbers during his residence in Egypt. On his return to Greece he established a school of occult philosophy that was eminently suited to the needs of his days. In this school only a very limited number of initiates were allowed to enter. The more involved and difficult the teachings became the fewer were the favoured ones who could boast that they were the—'chosen of the Master,' consequently a kind of occult hierarchy was established that raised an insurmountable barrier between these students and those they were pleased to call 'the common people.'

From this the most involved and complicated system of occult philosophy was launched: nothing was allowed to be put in writing, knowledge had to be handed down by word of mouth, and most elaborate ceremonials were instituted in which initiates were sworn to secrecy, and a lot of effort was made to conceal occult knowledge in every possible way.

After the death of Pythagoras, many of his followers started schools of philosophy of their own. All of them differed widely as to what 'the Master' really did teach. In the end confusion became still more confounded by the action of the early Fathers of the Christian Church condemning all occult learning as the 'work of the devil'.

One of the greatest of Pythagoras' teachings was that of the occult value of numbers. He laid down the axiom that numbers concealed and contained the secret of the universe. In this theory he was undoubtedly right, but his followers so complicated the rules he taught that in the end few could follow the great truth that underlay his wisdom.

In the study of numbers I advocate that the students should endeavour to get back to the original source; that is why I claim that in returning to the original Chaldean, Hindu, and Hebrew system, which I teach in my books, one has more likelihood of arriving at the real truth of such studies.

I could easily write an entire volume on the history of numbers, tracing its origin from the most remote ages; but in this practical period of humanity I realise that such an elaborate treatise is not required, that what men and women want is the practical appeal to their own personal experience and nothing more.

It is for this reason I have written this book for the masses, more than for the more limited erudite student.

Out of the many thousands of letters I have received, I shall now endeavour to answer those which appear to me as the most important.

Should the words Mr., Mrs. or Miss be calculated when working out the complete number of a name?'

Answer: As I have explained before, it is 'the name one is most known by' that should be used in working out the number of a name.

If, for example, a young lady is always addressed or spoken of as, say, Miss Jones—as is often the case in a large business establishment, then in connection *with that business* in which she is employed, Miss Jones should certainly take that name as the one she is most known by and work out the number of the name — 'Miss Jones' and use it, 'but only in relation to the business she is employed in.' It is in fact, her 'trade name' but for her home life or her private affairs she should work out the Christian name she is called by or the 'pet' name she is known by. When the same young lady enters the state of matrimony and becomes 'Mrs.' she should then work out the numbers for her new title, but always keeping the numbers of her Christian or 'pet' name *for her home and private life*. The same rule applies to every woman known and called continually 'Mrs. Smith' or 'Mrs. Jones,' as the case may be, in the circle of friends or acquaintances in which she is called 'Mrs.'

Men who have a business of their own or 'are working' in large establishments, who are generally called 'Mr.' before their name should also follow the above rule.

When a man or woman has many Christian names, they should only take the number made by the principle one—that they *are most known by*.

The same rule applies to every prefix or title a man or woman may obtain *by right of birth or as an honour.*

A good illustration of this is the case of the famous Melba.

The great diva's surname worked out to the compound number of 15, with 6 for the single, both being excellent for success. In one of my Press articles, speaking of the number 15, I said: "If this number is associated with a good or fortunate single number, it can be very lucky and powerful. It is peculiarly associated with 'good talkers' and often with gifts of eloquence, music, art and strong personal magnetism." All these qualities were characteristic of the great Melba, as she was called all through her successful career.

Her signature, Nellie Melba, produces the number 10, also a fortunate number, and the single number 1, is a number of strong individuality and ambition. It also denotes that people possessing this number have the desire to become the head or chief in whatever profession or occupation they take up.

If the number of her title, 'Dame,' which produces the lucky number 5, is added to the name Nellie Melba, the total of the last digits are :Dame 5, Nellie 4, Melba 6, giving the compound number 15 again, so that as long as this famous woman existed good fortune always favoured her.

I will now give an example of a title, which produces one of the unfortunate numbers, and the curious effect it foreshadows as far as the promise of good luck is concerned. In cases where the addition of the number of the title produces a 4 or an 8, it foreshadows that the fortunate numbers of the name have ceased their luck or power, and in such cases the title will become a detriment and not a happiness.

An illustration which may be given in connection with this is that of Napoleon. This name works out to the compound number of 41, which as I stated in my writings, is 'a magical number usually associated with combination of peoples or nations.' The single number is a 5, also fortunate. When Napoleon became the Emperor of France his name became Napoleon I, the I making his compound number 42 with the single number of 6. Both these numbers denote power and good fortune and he went down to posterity as the Great Napoleon.

In the case of Napoleon III the compound number becomes 44, which as I have I stated in my articles 'is a number of the gravest warnings for the future; it foreshadows disasters brought about by association with others and bad advice' — that is what exactly happened to Napoleon III. Again, 'the single number of his name become an 8 . Even the magic of the name Napoleon was overshadowed by it, and Napoleon III went down to posterity as 'the man who lost France'.

I think these illustrations will help to show how a prefix to a name or a title acquired or inherited, fits in with this wonderful science of Numerology, and the number it gives added to the other numbers is a further indication of good or evil fortune for the future.

The titles given to kings and queens when they ascend the throne, especially when taken in connection with their birth number, is generally very interesting.

In the case of King Edward VII, he changed his name when he came of the throne from Albert to Edward, the name he took worked out as follows:

```
King .................................. 11   =   2
Edward ........................... 22   =   4
VII ....................................      =   7
                                      ─────
                                         13
```

I have described this number in a previous chapter as a number of warning with its strange symbolism of 'a skeleton' or 'death'.

It was certainly a warning of great changes that was about to occur in England, especially when taken in conjunction with his birth number, November 9th. Adding the 4 produced by the 13 to the 9, they again made a 13, which doubled the warning and also indicated a short reign.

In the case of King George V, the numbers produced are as follows:

```
King .................................. 11   =   2
George ............................ 25   =   7
VII ....................................      =   5
                                      ─────
                                       14=5
```

The compound number 14 has already been described earlier as 'a number of movement, combinations of people and things, having danger from natural forces such as tempests, water, air or fire, and also having a strong element of risk and anger attached to it, generally owing to the actions and foolhardiness of others.'

The late king was born on June 3rd, in the Zodiacal Sign of Gemini, which is called the 1st House of Air. Consequently the dangers foreshown by the compound number of the name and title were all the more accentuated, therefore the king's greatest danger came from anything connected with air, even His Majesty's lungs, as the breathing apparatus of his system, came under this symbol of the Zodiacal Sign of Birth.

London, the capital of England, is also under the same sign of Gemini, and the greatest danger to it is from the air.

It is a curious fact, without doubt charged with deep significance that not only George V but Queen Mary and the Duke of Windsor were all born under the sign of Gemini or very close to it, in the 1st House of Air, and in the district of London, also under the same sign.

Although she had other Christian names, the Queen was always popularly known as Queen Mary. The numbers of her name are :

Queen 22	=	4
Mary	=	8
		12 = 3

The compound number of this name is 12. In my previous chapters I have given the symbolism of this number as 'a number indicating anxiety of mind.' It is also called 'the sacrifice.' As Queen Mary was born on May 26th, her birth number is an 8, and in the name Queen Mary, the numbers 4 and 8 are also produced.

I think, these illustrations of the significance of titles and prefixes to a name will be useful to my readers and will answer some thousands of letters I have received asking for information on this point.

Note : The Prince of Wales (The Duke of Windsor), born at 10 p.m., on June 23rd, 1894, in White Lodge, Richmond Park, London is in what is called the 'cusp' of Gemini-Cancer.

The sun at this date had just passed out of Gemini and was in 2 degrees 21 of Cancer. The qualities of Gemini will be the main influence through his life.

His Majesty King George V, born on June 3rd, 1865, at 1.18 am. in Marlborough House, London, has the sun in 12 degress 25 of Gemini.

Her Majesty Queen Mary, born on May 26th, 1867, at 11.59 p.m., in Kensington Palace, London, is in the 'cusp' of Taurus-Gemini and has the sun in 5 degress 13 of Gemini.

23. HOW TO FIND THE 'LUCKY' DAY

In answer to many letters, I take this opportunity of explaining a point of very great importance, namely, how to find the 'lucky' day.

I have stated that the birth number is the most important when the individuals wants *to carry out his own plans.*

For example : a person, for instance, born on the 1st of a month will find *for all general purposes* that if he or she will use all dates making the Number One series, such as the 1st, 10th, 19th or 28th of any month, especially during what is called the 'period of the 1' and the 'period of the 2,' namely, from June 21st to July 20th (period of the 2), and from July 21st to August 20th (period of the 1), they will have a far better chance of carrying out their plans successfully than if they did not follow this rule and did not know what dates to use for the best. This is quite independent of any other rule, and I strongly recommend it.

To get a still more powerful vibration, I have advised that persons should try to make the number of their name (when they have worked out the letters of it by what is called the Mystic or Ancient Hebrew Alphabet) in the same series as the number that is given by their birth date, and I have explained in a previous chapter how to do this by adding a letter to their name or taking away a letter, as the case may be. If these two numbers agree or are in harmony with one another, then they should use the date that is given to commence anything important or endeavour to carry out their plans on that number which is indicated. They must, however, bear in mind that any number of the series they belong to is equally important.

Example : The person born on the 1st of the month will find the 10th, 19th or 28th of equal importance to the number 1 on which they were born, and so on with every other birth number.

Naturally, when people begin to follow this idea, they must not expect to find their luck change in an instant, as if by magic. I have several letters before me, where the writers expected their luck to change for the better within twentyfour hours. There was one man who wrote that "at the end of a week he had found no change in his bad luck," but at the end of three months the same man again wrote to say that towards the middle of the third month he began to notice a distinct improvement in all his affairs.

Some of the writers have also apparently not grasped the example I gave in working out the number of the name of a man I called 'John Smith.' I stated in a previous chapter that if 'John Smith' wanted to find out a favourable date to ask his employer for an increase in his wages he should add the numbers given by the name 'John Smith' together, then add the single number of the date that he has in mind and lastly, add his Birth number. The result was a total of 15 as the last compound number with 6 as the last single number. Then look what number 15 symbolises, and you will find that it is a fortunate number for obtaining money, gifts, and favours from others. Therefore the date 'John Smith' wanted to see his employer would be a favourable date for him to make his request.

This was given only as an illustration of finding out if one particular date would be favourable *for that special purpose,* but I never intended this to be employed to the exculsion of the other definite rule for *continual action all through the year* on the series given by the Birth number, such as for a number 1 person to use all dates that make a 1, like the 1st, 10th, etc.

It will be noticed that in the latter case the rule is *individual or personal*; in the John Smith case another life, that of the employer, was also involved, and in consequence the rule given would not work out with such certainty.

24. COLOURS AND NUMBERS

There is no reason for anyone to get confused between the colours given by the number of month and those given by the number of the day, if one will bear in mind that the number of the month is not as *close or intimate in its relationship to the individual as is* the colour indicated by the number of birth.

Take the month of January, for example. The 'period of the number 8' as set out in Chapter 11 is from December 21st to January 20th *in its positive aspect*, and from January 21st to February 20th *in its negative aspect*. The number 8 as I have already stated, has for its colours 'all shades of dark grey, dark blue and purple.' In this work on Numerology I have simply condensed the colours for the number 8 people to what are called 'half shades, half tones or electric colours,' and have stated that 'electric blues' and greys seem to suit them best of all. In all this there is no contradiction of terms, as the writers of many letters to me appear to imagine. There are so many sides to the study of the occult value of numbers that one cannot put all the information in one book.[1]

I think, the following information will be useful, and I am giving it in order to clear up a point which I have noticed in many of the letters that have been received.

A person born on, say January 6th will find that January is the 'period of 8,' and that the colours for the number 8 are 'all tones of grey, all ranges of violet and purple, also black.' Many of those who have written to me are puzzled to know whether they should use the colours of the 8 or those belonging to the number 6. My answer is, employ *most decidedly in such a case* the colours of the number 6 as the principal, individual, and 'lucky' colours to use, but as the person was born in the 'period of the 8' he or she can use, if they wish, but *as secondary* colours, those given by the number 8.

---

[1] The deep-toned sapphire is also principal jewel of the number 4, and all its series.

Another illustration I will give is for those born in the 'period of 9,' namely between March 21st and April 27th, which is the *positive period of 9*, and those born *in its negative period*, namely between October 21st and November 27th.

If one will look up the colours I have given earlier to the number 9, they will find that they are all shades of crimson or red, 'all rose tones and pink' for the *positive period*, while for the *negative period* October-November, one will notice that I advised "all shades of *crimson and blue.*"

Where does blue come in ? one may ask.

It comes in because the opposite Sign of the Zodiac to the period October 21st to November 27th is what is called 'the House of Venus' in her positive aspect, and as Venus which is also the number 6, represents in this wonderful colour scheme of Nature all shades of blue, these blue rays appear to cross from one side of the Zodiac to the other and so become a favourable colour for persons born in the *negative period of the number* 9, alongwith 'all shades of crimson.'

Going back to the 'period of the number 9' for a month we find the basic colours for both these periods are red, crimson, and pink, but the same rule applies as it did in my example for the 'period of the 8.' A person born on a 6, such as on the 6th, 15th or 24th *in the period of the 9*, would have as his or her *principal colour* all shades of blue, with red, crimson or pink, as his or her *secondary colours.*

The same rule applies to every month in the year and to every date of birth. It is quite simple when one has once grasped this principle and can appreciate the marvellous harmony of this wonderful universe in which we live.

25. THE VALUE OF CONCENTRATION IN REGARD TO ONE'S NUMBER

In order to help my readers to make the best of whatever their number may be, I will now give an advice which I am sure will be of great assistance to those who want to try make the most out of their lives.

Once the principal or dominating number of the life has been found, then the next step *is to increase its power as much as possible,* the exception being those who are born under the 8, namely the 8th, 17th or 28th of any month, to whom I will give advice on this point later.

This increase of power can be obtained by employing one of the *greatest forces* that man is endowed with, namely the Power of Concentration. There are very few people who know anything about this extraordinary power.

All successful men and women are endowed with it, many use it unconsciously. Some are born with it, others develop it, but the majority of mankind do not use it at all.

One may often have noticed the feeble, 'wishy-washy' way most people talk. One may have tried hard to follow some rambling statement, but have found at the end that one hardly follows 'what it was all about,' or that the person who has tried to interest you has made no impression on you whatsoever. This has been due to the fact that the man or woman has no power of concentration, and consequently *no force behind their flow of words.*

It is the same when such people write a letter—again there may be a lot of words, even expressions and sentences well put together, but the letter has no *effect on you,* and its very likely that you toss it aside and think no more about it.

On the contrary, another person may say only a few words, but *those words have effect;* or they may write, and their sentences strike home—the secret of this mystery is *concentration of mind.*

The simplest way of developing this power is by the use of numbers. I will now explain.

The first thing to be done is to find one's own number, the birth number being in every case the simplest and the most certain; the next is to grasp *the meaning of that number,* and lastly, to think of oneself as if that number *belonged* to one, represented one, and were *part and parcel of ones aims and plans.*

This is the basic foundation on which to build the other aspects.

We will now proceed to step farther. The man or woman who has found his own distinct number should plan with firm determination to use that number in every way possible.

They should mentally look forward to the day or date when their number is to appear and plan that *on that day* they will take a certain course of action, and when that day or date arrives they will go straight for what they want without shilly-shallying or hesitation of any kind.

Having read previous chapters on numbers, the reader has by now grasped the characteristics of other persons that are born under their own or other numbers. It is quite a simple matter to find out the day of the month on which the person one is going to interview was born, for if one does not ask the year of birth, even the woman most sensitive about her age will tell the date on which she was born.

A number 1 person will realise how useless it is to attempt to dominate a number 3 person. On the contrary, they must appeal to their ambition, their conscientiousness in carrying out their duties, their love of order and discipline, their sense of independence and the pride of honour and self, that is the foundation principle of the number 3 person.

If they bear this in mind, *concentrating at the same time on their own plan* that made them seek the interview they will find that the number 3 person, instead of being difficult to approach, will, on the contrary, be willing to help and will most probably give ideas and suggestions that will be useful.

Having chosen a date for the interview on *one of their own numbers* and by doing so, having concentrated their mind on this plan of action, they will find how easily they will be able to influence the person they have come to interview.

26. COMBINATION BETWEEN '1-4' PERSONS AND UNIQUENESS OF THE NUMBERS 4 AND 8

Following the illustrations I gave in the previous chapters on the usefulness of concentration on one's own number, so as to increase its power (except in case of those born under the 4 and 8), we will now take as an example a number 1 person meeting another of his own number. My readers have already learned from previous chapters that people born on the same series are naturally sympathetic to one another, and such knowledge gives the feeling in the first place that the other number 1 he is talking to is 'one of themselves,' as it were. This very sentiment radiating outwards destroys nervousness and allows the lines of human magnetism to vibrate in harmony from one to the other.

Let us now suppose that the number 1 person has arranged an interview with an individual born under the 2 series. In such a case he or she can select any date of the 1 or 2 series, such as the 1st, 2nd, 10th, 11th, 19th, 20th, 28th or 29th. The number 1 person has read that number 2 persons have the feminine qualities of the number 1, and that, though opposite in character, the vibrations of both 1 and 2 persons are harmonious, and that they make good combinations. With this knowledge in his possession the number 1 person will make the effort to combine with the ideas of number 2, and so happy and good results will be obtained.

A number 1 and a number 4 person will also meet on sympathetic and harmonious vibration for the reason that in Numerology the number 1 is always associated with 4 and these numbers are written as '1-4' and '4-1', but as all number 4 persons have a very decided individuality, they must not be subjugated by the number 1 person but must be allowed to keep their own distinct character and to see things from their own point of view. If the number 1 person will keep the peculiar temperament of the number 4 in mind, any combination with a number 4 person should be most successful.

In order to achieve success, the basic requirement, as I have already suggested at the commencement, is the development of the power of concentration *on one's own number*, so as to *increase its influence*. This holds good for all born under all other numbers except for numbers 4 and 8.

In previous chapters I have already warned all those under the 4's and 8's, such as the persons born on the 4th, 8th, 13th, 17th, 22nd, 26th, and 31st to avoid all numbers making an 8 or a 4 as much as possible; not to live in houses that have such numbers, and not to choose dates that make them.

In the preceding pages I have already gone into fuller details regarding the 4 and 8 series, but let me once again put the rules to be followed by them briefly.

Never increase the power of these numbers. Consequently they must not follow the rule laid down for those born under the other numbers, but on the contrary they should do the very opposite.

As they cannot alter their Birth number, they can alter the number made by their name and cause it to produce one of the more fortunate series, especially one of a strong vibration such as a 1, 3, 5 or 6. Having definitely fixed in this way that they are going *to be represented* by the strong number they have made out of their name, they should then follow the rule I gave previously, namely, *think of themselves as that number* and do everything that is important on dates that make the number. If they do this, *and do it persistently,* the number 4 or 8 persons will get away from the bad luck that they are prone to experience and so become as equally fortunate as others.

They must not, however, expect the change to be seen in a few days, as so many in their impatience do, but in a reasonable space of time they will see very marked results in their favour.

27. MORE ABOUT PERSONS BORN UNDER THE NUMBERS 4 AND 8

I have received so many letters from numbers 4 and 8 people, asking for advice, that I think it will be useful to devote an entire chapter to such cases.

Out of every hundred letters, eighty write fully testifying to the accuracy of my system of numbers, especially regarding the hard luck that appears to pursue persons who have the combination of 4 and 8 continually cropping up in their lives.

The 4 itself and all its series should not be dreaded so much. Persons born on the 4th, 13th, 22nd, and 31st will find these dates and numbers the most important in their lives, but as the 4 in Numerology is always associated with the number 1, and in nearly all systems is written as '4-1' or '1-4', and as 1 is a strong and powerful number, — I advise the number 4 persons to use *'the strong number'* as much as possible and select all dates such as the 1st, 10th, 19th, and 28th, for their most important efforts, and to endeavour to live in houses whose number or the addition of whose number makes a number 1. They should also remember that as what is called the interchangeable numbers of the '1-4' series are the '2-7' and all their series, they need not be afraid of such dates or numbers as the 2nd, 6th, 11th, 16th, 20th, 25th or 29th.

It is only when the combination of the 4 and 8 *are continually cropping* up that those born under such number should do their utmost to avoid them.

Example : A man born on either the 4th, 13th, 22nd or 31st marries a woman born on either the 8th, 17th or 26th. He will most certainly find that 4's and 8's will influence his life more than any other number, generally bringing sadness, ill-luck or terrible blows of fate in their train. So, such people should definitely avoid using all 4's and 8 and use the number 1 series instead, and for the next best use the '2-7' series.

For some reason, due probably to some law of magnetic vibration, 4 and 8 people generally attract one another, but from *a purely worldly* standpoint the combination cannot be considered lucky. They often show the highest devotion to one another during illness and misfortune, and some of the greatest examples of self-sacrifice are found when 4's and 8's marry or make a combination together.

Number 8 person belong to a still more fatalistic law of vibration and appear to be children of fate more than any other class.

They can be just as noble in character, as devoted and self-sacrificing as the best of their fellow beings, but *they seldom get the reward that they are entitled to.* If they rise in life to any high position it is generally one of grave responsibility, anxiety, and care. Such persons can become rich, but wealth seldom brings them happiness, and for love they are generally called on to pay too high a price.

My advice to them is: If they find the 4's and 8's continually coming into their lives and associated with sorrow, disappointment, ill-fate, and ill-luck, they should determinately avoid such numbers and all their series. They should, in such a case, so alter their name number, following the example I have given in previous chapters, to produce one of the more fortunate series, such as a 1, 3, 5 or 6, and carry out their plans on dates that make these numbers. If they will do this they will completely alter their ill-luck and control, as it were, the curious fate that appears to follow them.

If, however, they prefer, as many do, to carry out the *full force and meaning of their number 8,* without caring what the wordly result may be, in that case they should do exactly as I have said for the other numbers and do everything important on dates and numbers that make the 8, such as the 8th, 17th, 26th, also the 4th, 13th, 22nd, and 31st.

If they do this they will be equally successful, but in leading peculiarly fatalistic lives, they would be the, 'marked' or the 'selected few' people in whatever path of life they may make.

Many have written to ask how to change from an unlucky or fatalistic set of number to more fortunate ones. This question is generally asked by people who are born under the series of 4's and 8's, and who have proved, as I have said, that all combinations of such numbers have been more or less associated with fatalistic events in the life. In such cases, when persons are born on the 4th, 13th, 22nd or 31st in any month they should try to avoid doing important things on dates making the 8 or any of its combinations, such as the 8th, 17th, 26th, and *take instead the number 1 series or the number of the Zodiacal period of the month they are born in.* For example: A person born between February

19th and March 20th being in the *period of 3*, if they happen to be born on February 22nd or 26th or on March 4th, 8th, 13th, 17th or 22nd, will find it more lucky for them to use the 3 series instead of their birth number, the 4 or 8. In fact, in such cases it will be better for them to drop the birth number altogether.

The same rule will apply to all the other month periods of the year *with the exception of the period* from December 21st to January 20th, the period of the number 8 positive, and from January 21st to February 19th, the period of number 8 negative. If born in these two periods the 4 and 8 people *must not select the number of the month period,* because if they did they would only increase the power of the 4 and 8. I advise them in such cases to take the number of the month period *exactly opposite to their Zodiac period,* which is : For December 21st to January 20th, the opposite numbers are those of June 21st to July 20th, which, if they refer to Chapter 11 of this book, they will find is the period of the 2-7. For people born between January 21st to February 19th, the opposite period of the Zodiac is July 31st to August 20th, the number of which are 1-4. By following this rule all people who have 4 and 8 as their birth number will be able to select numbers to be used in place of the series of their 4 and 8, and by employing the new numbers, will, in a short time, begin to notice how much more fortunate their lives have become.

They should employ also the colours and jewels which their *new numbers indicate* instead of those given for the 4's and 8's.

I feel sure this information will be useful to many hundreds who have asked questions on this extremely important point.

Many number 2 persons have written and asked me why it is that apart from their own numbers—2, 11, 20, and 29th, the number 8 also appear to have a great importance in their lives. The reason for this is that 8, being a very strong number with a fatalistic tendency, tries to dominate the weaker number 2, which has a relation to itself as 4 times 2 is 8, but 8 is not a happy combination when it comes into the lives of number 2 persons, and it should always be regarded as a warning of sorrow and disappointment or fatalistic experiences of some kind.

The 4 will also be found to have a great deal of influence with number 2 persons, but this is because it not only represents the double of the number 2, but it is also one of the interchangeable numbers, such as 1 and 4 are the interchageable numbers of the 2 and 7.

28. THE AFFINITY OF COLOURS AND NUMBERS AND HOW MUSIC AND NUMBERS ARE ASSOCIATED

Number 1 persons, namely those born on the 1st, 10th, 19th or 28th (numbers which by the addition of themselves produce the number 1), should dress themselves as much as possible in all shades of brown (light or dark) and all shades of yellow or gold colours or at least have some of these colours about their person. If they have the freedom to select colours for their sleeping rooms, they should follow the same rule.

They will find this colour rule will have an excellent effect in soothing their nerves, and they will rest and sleep better in rooms having their own colours.

Number 2 persons, namely those born on the 2nd 11th, 20th or 29th, should wear all shades of green from the darkest to the lightest shade, also cream and white. They should avoid all heavy dark colours especially black, purple, and dark red.

Number 3 persons, namely those born on the 3rd, 12th, 21st or 30th, should wear shades of mauve, violet or the pale or lilac shades or purple, but as men cannot easily dress in such colours, they should at least employ them in the neckties, shirts or handkerchiefs.

Number 4 persons, namely those born on the 4th, 13th, 22nd or 31st, should wear what are called the 'electric colours,' blue, greys, electric blues, and what are known as 'half shades.' They should avoid strong or positive colours of all kinds.

Number 5 persons, namely, those born on the 5th, 14th or 23rd, should wear the light shades of all colours especially light greys, white and glistening materials. They should never wear dark colours if they can possibly avoid doing so.

Number 6 persons, namely, those born on the 6th, 15th or 24th, should wear all shades of blue, from the lightest to the dark navy, what is known as the full or real blue, not 'electric blue.' For secondary colours, they can also wear shades of rose or pink, but not red, scarlet or crimson, unless they are born between March 21st and April 24th or between October 21st and November 24th.

Number 7 persons, namely, those born on the 7th, 16th or 25th, should, like the number 2 persons wear all shades of pale green, white, yellow, and gold colours. The palest possible shades are best for them, such as what are known as 'pastel shades'.

Number 8 persons, namely, those born on the 8th, 17th or 26th, should wear all shades of dark grey, dark blue, purple, and black; light and gaudy colours are out of place with them and should be avoided.

Number 9 persons, namely, those born on 9th, 18th or 27th, should wear all shades of red, rose crimson, pink or red purple. The darker or rich shades of these colours are best for them.

Red is the colour of the soldier, the colour of energy, restlessness and revolution. It is the chosen colour of the Revolutionist and Anarchist; hence, the origin of the 'red' flag.

On account of the magnetic rays sent off by a number 9 person, their presence often irritates people belonging to other numbers, except those born under the number 1, the 3, the 5, the 6 or their own number. People born under the other numbers are very nervous or uncomfortable in the presence of a number 9 person.

Numbers and music show very decided affinities. The number 1, 3, and 9 persons like martial, inspiring or what may be called 'full-blooded' tones; number 2 and 7 persons, are more partial to string and wind instruments, such as the violin, cello, harp, pipes, etc. Number 6 persons like romantic, sweet music of all kinds with a lilt and rhythm; number 5 persons lean towards either extremely original or unusual music, something off the beaten track.

Number 4 and 8 persons, if musical, have a special leaning for the organ and make magnificent choir or choral leaders, but in all their music there is an undertone of plaintiveness, melancholy, religious fervour or fatalism.

The following are a few examples of countries having their own individual or what is called National Music, in accordance with the planet and number by which they are governed.

England and Germany, governed by Mars (number 9), martial, inspiring or full-blooded music.

Ireland, governed by Venus (number 6), romantic, sweet music, with a lilt or rhythm.

Scotland, governed by the Moon (number 2) and Saturn (number 8), string and wind instruments.

Wales, governed by Uranus (number 4) and Mercury (number 5), original music, with undertone of religious fervour, melancholy, choral and choir.

The United States, governed by the Planet Mercury (number 5), can use the qualities of that number and adapt itself to all types of music, but will always lean to what is original new, and out of the ordinary—hence this country is the natural birthplace of what is called jazz or syncopated music.

29. NUMBERS AND DISEASE : PLANETARY SIGNIFICANCE OF HERBAL CURES

In some press articles I gave an account of the various diseases that are associated with persons born under the numbers that make their birth date. I have received so many letters testifying to the accuracy of this system and begging me to give further information as to indications from occultism regarding the cure of diseases, that I have much pleasure in giving in this chapter the name of herbs that are beneficial to persons born under the different numbers.

To keep in good health is one of the essentials to achieve success in life, and by following my advice I am sure that my readers would gain much benefit.

The same students of occultism who discovered the extraordinary influence of numbers in connection with the destiny of individuals, also discovered the sympathy of certain plants, fruits, and herbs that in the world of Nature are related to the planets and months of the year in which people are born, and so evolved a system by which pain and illness can be alleviated by the use of such herbs or fruits which correspond to each planet and consequently to the number of birth.

I have collected this information from some of the most ancient sources of knowledge of occultism and from those who have devoted their lives to the investigation of the subject. To this I have added my own lifelong experience, in the belief that by the study of Nature we may find the secrets of Nature.

Number 1 person or all those born on the 1st, 10th, 19th, and 28th, of any month, have a tendency to suffer from the heart in some form or another, such as palpitation, irregular circulation, and in advanced life, high blood-pressure. They are also likely to have trouble with the eyes or astigmatism, and would do well to have their sight carefully tested from time to time.

The principal herbs and fruits for number 1 persons or all those born on the 1st, 10th, 19th or 28th, are: Raisins, camomile, eye-bright, St. John's wort, saffron, cloves, nutmeg, sorrel, borage, gentian root, lavender, bay leaves, oranges, lemons, dates, thyme, myrrh, musk, vervain, ginger, barley (barley bread and barley water). Number 1 persons should eat honey as much as possible.

They will find that their nineteenth, twenty-eighth, thirty-seventh, and fifty-fifth years will bring about important changes in health one way or the other.

The months to be most guarded against for ill-health and overwork are : October, December, and January.

Number 2 persons or all those born on the 2nd, 11th, 20th or 29th have a tendency to suffer with the stomach and digestive organs.

The principal herbs for number 2 persons or those born on the 2nd, 11th, 20th or 29th of any month are: Lettuce, cabbages, turnips, cucumber, melon, chicory or endive, rapeseed, colewort, moonwort, linseed, water plantain, and ash of willow.

They will find the twentieth, twenty-fifth, twenty-ninth, forty-third, forty-seventh, fifty-second, and sixty-fifth years will bring them important changes in health. The three months to be most guarded against for ill-health and overwork are January, February, and July.

Number 3 persons or all those born on the 3rd, 12th, 21st or 30th have a tendency to suffer from overstrain of the nervous system, generally brought on by overwork and their desire not to spare themselves in anything they do.

They are inclined to have attacks of neuritis and sciatica, and also many forms of skin troubles.

The principal herbs for number 3 persons or those born on the 3rd, 12th or 30th of any month, are beets, borage, bilberries, asparagus, dandelion, endive, ewewort, lungwort, sage, cherries, barberries, strawberries, pomegranates, pineapples, grapes, mint, saffron, nutmegs, cloves, sweet marjoram, St. John's wort, almonds, figs, hazel-nuts, and wheat.

The months to be most guarded against for ill-health and overwork are December, February, June and September. The important years for changes in health are the twelfth, twenty-first, thirty-ninth, forty-eighth, and fifty-seventh.

Number 4 persons or all those born on the 4th, 13th, 22nd or 31st, have a likelihood of suffering from mysterious ailments, difficult to be diagnosed in an ordinary manner. They are more or less inclined to melancholia, anaemia and pains in the head and back.

The principal herbs for number 4 persons or those born on the 4th, 13th, 22nd or 31st of a month, are spinach, sage, pilewort, wintergreen, medlars, icelandmoss, and Solomon's seal. Number 4 persons derive the greatest benefit from electric treatment of all kinds, mental suggestion, and hypnotism. They should be particularly careful to avoid drugs, also highly seasoned dishes and red meat.

The months to be guarded against for ill-health and overwork are January, February, July, August, and September.

The important years for their health are the thirteenth, twenty-second, thirty-first, fortieth, forty-ninth, and fifty-eighth.

Number 5 persons or all those born on the 5th, 14th or 23rd, have a tendency to overstrain the nervous system. They are inclined to attempt too much mentally, to live too much on their nerves. They are likely to bring on such things as neuritis and are prone to nervous prostration and insomnia. Sleep, rest, and quietude are the best medicines they can employ.

The principal herbs for number 5 persons or those born on the 5th, 14th or 23rd of any month, are carrots, parsnips, seakale, oats in the form of oatmeal or bread, parsley, sweet marjoram, champignons, caraway seeds, thyme, nuts of all kinds but especially hazel-nuts and walnuts.

The months to be most guarded against for ill-health and overwork are June, September, and December.

The important years for changes in their health are the fourteenth, twenty-third, forty-first, and the fiftieth.

Number 6 persons or all those born on the 6th, 15th, 24th, are inclined to suffer with the throat, nose and upper part of the lungs. As a rule they have a strong robust constitution, especially if they can live in the open or in the country, where they can have plenty of air and exercise. Women born under the number 6 often suffer with their breasts. The heart as a general rule becomes affected in the latter years and produces irregular circulation of the blood.

The herbs for number 6 persons or those born on the 6th, 15th or 24th of any month, are all kinds of beans, parsnip, spinach, marrow, mint, melon, motherwort, pomegranate, apple, peach, apricots, figs, walnuts, almonds and the juice of maidenhair-fern, daffodils, wild thyme, musk, violets, vervain, and rose leaves.

The months to be most guarded against for ill-health and overwork are May, October and November.

They will find that the fifteenth, twenty-fourth, forty-second, fifty-first and sixtieth years will bring them important changes in health.

Number 7 persons or those who are born on the 7th, 16th or 25th, are more easily affected by worry and annoyance than any other class. As long as things are going smoothly, they can get through any amount of work, but if worried, either by circumstances or people, they are inclined to imagine that things are worse than they are and get easily despondent and melancholic.

They are extremely sensitive to their surroundings; they will gladly accept any responsibility for those who appear to appreciate them; they are unusually conscientious in doing any work that is interesting to them, but as they are more stronger mentally than physically, they often have frail bodies that attempt too much for their strength. They are inclined to have some peculiar delicacy in connection with the skin; it is either extremely sensitive to friction or has some peculiarity as regards perspiration.

The principal herbs for number 7 persons or those born on the 7th, 16th or 25th of any month, are lettuce, cabbage, chicory or endive, cucumber, colewort, linseed, mushrooms, ceps, sorrel, apples, grapes and the juice of all fruits. The months to be most guarded against for ill-health and overwork are January, February, July and August.

The most important years for changes in health are the seventh, sixteenth, twenty-fifth, thirty-fourth, forty-third, fifty-second, and sixty-first.

Number 8 persons or those born on the 8th, 17th or 26th, are as a rule liable to have trouble with the liver, bile and intestines. They are prone to suffer with headaches and rheumatism. They should avoid animal food as much as possible and live on fruits, herbs, and vegetables.

The principal herbs for number 8 persons or those born on the 8th, 17th or 26th of any month, are spinach, winter green, angelica, wild carrot, marshmallow, plantain, sage, pilewort, ragwort, shepherd's purse, Solomon's seal, vervain, elder flowers, gravel root, mandrake root, celery.

The months to be most guarded against for ill-health and effects of overwork are December, January, February, and July. They will find the most important years for changes in health are the seventeenth, twenty-sixth, thirty-fifth, forty-fourth, fifty-third, and sixty-second.

Number 9 persons or those born on the 9th, 18th or 27th, are more or less inclined to fevers of all kinds, measles, chicken-pox, scarlatina, and such-like. They should avoid rich food, also alcoholic drinks or wines.

The principal herbs for number 9 persons or those born on the 9th, 18th or 27th of any month, are onions, garlic, leeks, horse-radish, rhubarb, mustard-seed, wormwood, betony, spear-wort, white hellebore, ginger, pepper, broom, rape, madder, hops, danewort, and juice of nettles.

The months to be most guarded against for ill-health or the effects of overwork are April, May, October and November.

They will find the most important years for changes in the health are the ninth, eighteenth, twenty-seventh, thirty-sixth, forty-fifth, and sixty-third.

The herbs that have been mentioned in these pages can be obtained from all good herbalists in almost all countries. Herbs are Nature's own remedies.

30. HOW TO KNOW WHAT CITY, TOWN OR PLACE IS FORTUNATE FOR ONE TO LIVE IN

In this chapter I intend to show how each person may more easily find if any city, town or place is in a harmonious vibration with themselves.

Such information should be of great value to those who find; as so many do, that certain town or place has proved to be unfortunate; they may desire to make a change, but as they have nothing to guide them, they do not know what to do or how to arrive at a decision. The following rules will, I believe, be of great help to all such people.

Taking the numbers 1 to 9 as the foundation numbers, which by now all those readers who have followed this book will know are the basic numbers by which all calculation on this earth is founded, I will therefore give example of how each birth number may be found in any city, town or place.

Work out the numbers of the name of the city or town by the numbers given to each letter by the Mystic Alphabet which I have given in Chapter 13. Put these numbers under each letter and add them together until only one figure remains; if this single number corresponds to the birth number, then the vibrations of that city, town or place will accord with the individual, and the district indicated by the number should be fortunate for the person whose birth number corresponds with it, and still more so if the person's name number is also in accord.

Number 1 persons, such as all those born on the 1st, 10th, 19th or 28th, would therefore find the following towns more likely to be favourable. We will take Manchester, as an example. The name works out as follows:

MANCHESTER
4 1 5 3 5 5 3 4 5 2 = 37 and 3 plus 7
                         = 10 or the single number 1.

Other towns that make the number 1 are :
    Birmingham 1
    Boston 1
    New York 1

Alexandria 1
Whitechapel 1

There are many other places that will produce the number 1 by this system.

Number 1 and 4 and number 2 and 7 persons have a greater choice than those born under any of the other numbers, for, as I have previously explained in my chapter on this subject, number 1 belongs to the '1-4' series whose interchangeable or sympathetic numbers are the '2-7' series; therefore number 1, 2, 4 or 7 persons could select all places that give as their single number any of the series of 1, 2, 4 and 7.

Number 2 persons or all those born on the 2nd, 11th, 20th or 29th, can select any town whose final number makes any one of the above series, but more especially a town making their own series of the 2. We will take as an example:

L E E D S
3 5 5 4 3 = 20 = 2

or any of the following places which all total to the number 2 :

Plymouth 2
Los Angeles 2
Norwich 2
Brighton 2

Number 3 persons or all those born on the 3rd, 12th, 21st or 30th, can take as an example :

C R E W E
2 3 5 6 5 = 21 = 3

or any of the following towns which add to produce number 3, such as:

Dublin 3
Bath 3
Reading 3
Limerick 3
Moscow 3
Melbourne 3
York 3
Nottingham 3
Devonport 3
Bradford 3

Number 4 persons or all those born on the 4th, 13th, 22nd or 31st, can take as an example :

L O N D O N
3 7 5 4 7 5 = 31 = 4

or any of the following towns which add to the number 4, such as:

Paisley	4
Bristol	4
Leicester	4
Quebec	4
Montreal	4
Stockport	4
Salisbury	4

or any town indicated by the numbers of the 1, 2, 4 or 7 series as I have explained earlier.

Number 5 persons or all those born on the 5th, 14th or 23rd, can take as an example :

T A U N T O N
4 1 6 5 4 7 5 = 32 = 5

or any of the following towns which makes number 5, such as:

Southport	5
Portsmouth	5
Chicago	5
Cork	5
Vienna	5

But as the number 5 is the only number that can associate or harmonise with any other number, they need not be so careful as to what place they select, for as they can get on with persons born under any other number almost equally as well as with those born under their own, so in the same way they get on equally well in any city or place no matter what its number may be.

Number 6 persons or all those born on the 6th, 15th or 24th, can take as an example :

L I V E R P O O L
3 1 6 5 2 8 7 7 3 = 42 = 6

or any of the following towns, which adds to number 6, such as:

Edinburgh	6
Swansea	6
Paris	6

Dover	6
Worthing	6
Halifax	6
Oxford	6
Cologne	6
San Francisco	6
Cowes	6
Sheffield	6

Number 7 persons or all those born on the 7th, 16th or 25th, can take as an example :

W I G A N
6 1 3 1 5 = 16 = 7

or any of the following towns which adds to number 7, such as:

Doncaster	7
Hollywood	7
Whitehaven	7
Auckland	7
Calcutta	7
Tiverton	7
Grimsby	7
Preston	7

or any town indicated by the number of the 1, 2, 4, 7 series, as I explained earlier.

Number 8 persons or all those born on the 8th, 17th or 26th, can take as an example :

G L A S G O W
3 3 1 3 3 7 6 = 26 = 8

or any of the following , such as :

Belfast	8
Stoke-on-Trent	8
Hull	8
Bombay	8
Bournemouth	8

But, as I have already explained, I advise all number 4 and 8 persons not to increase the influence of the number 8 by employing or living under this strangely fatalistic number, but instead to make their name number work out to a more fortunate vibration, such as those of the 1, 3, 5 or 6 series.

Number 9 persons or all those born on the 9th, 18th or 27th, can take as an example :

W O L V E R H A M P T O N
6 7 3 6 5 2 5 1 4 8 4 7 5 = 63 = 9

or any of the following towns which add to form number 9, such as:

Blackpool 9
Whitehead 9
St. Louis 9
Berlin 9
Rome 9
Toronto 9
Brussels 9

As I have explained previously, the series of 3, 6, 9, if added together in any direction, produce a 9 as their final digit, so the persons born under any one of these series will find others born under any of these series sympathetic to them, so they can take any city or town whose final number makes a 3, 6, 9, as if they used only their own individual number.

In conclusion, it should be borne in mind that towns and places should be regarded as the *larger octave of harmony,* the number of one's house *the more intimate,* the number of the date and day of the week *the more immediate as regards events,* and the birth number of persons in relation to oneself as *the more personal* as regards our feelings, affections, and home life.

If this is borne in mind, the reason and logic of this special system of Numerology is easily seen, and the harmony it makes for becomes apparent to every student of humanity.

31. HORSE-RACING AND NUMBERS

I have received so many letters asking for information as to how my system of numbers could be employed in 'betting,' that I cannot conclude this book without trying to give some advice on a subject that is of interest to so many thousands.

There is no doubt that the study of numbers can open up a new field for the successful backing of horses, but there is no saying more true than—'a little knowledge is a dangerous thing.'

My experience is that people are too much inclined to think that because they have proved that the system I teach has such a bearing on the leading events in their own individual lives, that without more preparation they are ready to plunge into racing and back any horse whose name makes the same numbers as their own.

The point so many people seem to forget is that horse-racing is an extremely complicated business, so much so that 'tips,' even from owners and jockeys, are as a rule as equally unreliable as the hundred and one systems that are offered daily to the public by almost every newspaper that one picks up.

Many important racing events have upset all theories as to forecasting the winner by a study of 'form,' previous running, and so forth. At many races complete outsiders have, for no apparent reason, beaten the most heavily backed favourites.

Can the study of numbers be used to give a clear indication of which horses are likely to be first, second, and third ?

I say most emphatically that it can, but the trouble is that it is so rare to find persons who can 'keep their heads' when it comes to such a thing as a *systematic employment of any method,* and more particularly with numbers.

If one really made up one's mind to experiment with the system of numbers as set out in these pages in connection with betting, one would have to do it on the following lines:

To attend the race meeting in person.

Select a day whose number accords with one's own.

If possible, find out the jockeys whose birth number is the same as the number of the day.

When all these numbers are in accord, say, for example, if they all worked out to a number, such as the 9, then such horses, if they run under the number 9, 18, and 27 on that day would certainly be more likely to come in as first, second, and third than any others.

In such a case it would be necessary to back the three horses that are to run under the numbers 9, 18, and 27 on the starting board for 'win and place.' If there were a greater number than 36 running in the race it would be necessary also to take in the horse under that number, but if too much money would be at stake by backing all four, a good rule is to select *the two youngest horses* out of the four and back these two for 'win and place.' If there were not much difference in age, the next rule to employ is to select the *youngest male horse* in preference to *the youngest female*. If on the first race one lost, on the following race the stakes should be doubled, and so on systematically during the day. If this plan were carried out and the numbers selected steadfastly adhered to, one would sooner or later be rewarded by a first, second or it may be all three, with the added chance of getting a complete outsider in some of the events.

The greatest difficulty is that a very few people at a race meeting have sufficient strength of will to follow such a plan systematically. They may try it for one race and because they have not met with immediate success, they are likely to do nothing for the next event or plunge after some 'tip' they were given, and so on.

To those who are unable to attend the race meeting personally, my advise is not to try to 'find the winner' by numbers, for the simple reason that if they have not got *the running number of the horse* they miss one of the principal elements for success.

32. NAMES AND NUMBERS OF SOME OF THE USA HEADS

In this chapter, let me further clarify the concept of names and numbers by citing the name of some the popular Presidents of the United States.

GEORGE WASHINGTON

In taking illustrations from the names of Presidents of the United States, I cannot do better than start with the name of George Washington.

```
G E O R G E     W A S H I N G T O N
3 5 7 2 3 5     6 1 3 5 1 5 3 4 7 5
-----------     -------------------
    2 5                 4 0
    ---                 ---
     7             4 = 11 = 2
```

The number of the famous name of George Washington, the first President of the United States, worked out by the Chaldean or Hebrew alphabet, as set out in the example on Lloyd George, gives to the name GEORGE the compound number of 25, with its single and final digit of 7. On looking up the meaning of the compound number of 25 in Chapter 14, it will be found stated :

This is a number denoting strength gained through experience and benefits obtained through observation of people and things. It is not deemed exactly 'lucky,' as its success is given through strife and trials in the earlier life. It is favourable when it appears in regard to the future.

The word WASHINGTON works out to the compound number of 30, with its single digit of 4.

The meaning of this compound number is given in Chapter 14 as :

This is a number of thoughtful deduction, retrospection, and mental superiority over one's fellows, but, as it seems to belong to the mental plane, it represents people who are likely to put all material things on one side, not because they have to, but because they wish to do so.

This is remarkably borne out by Washington's resignation of the position of the Commander-in-Chief of the victorious American Army when he met his assembled Generals for the last time. His own words were, "With heart full of love and gratitude, I now take leave of you."

Addressing the President of Congress, Washington said—"the great events on which my resignation depended having, at length, taken place, I have now the honour to surrender into their [Congress's] hands the trust committed to me and to claim the indulgence of retiring from the service of my country. Having now finished the work assigned me, I retire."

The really great man, so justly called the 'Father of the United States,' refused to accept any reward for his long years of arduous service, and thus retired to his home at Mount Vernon.

The distinguished name of George Washington bears out in a remarkable manner the occult meaning of the numbers of this name.

If the final digits of 7 for GEORGE and 4 for WASHINGTON be added together they produce eleven (11), with the single digit of 2. This compound number 11, on being raised to its higher octave, 20, gives for this compound number (see Chapter 14) the symbol of 'The Awakening,' also the 'The Judgement,' with the interpretation—the awaken ng of new purpose, new plans, new ambitions, the call to action, but for some great purpose, cause or duty.

It will thus be seen from this example how wonderfully this system of Numerology fits in with and explains the underlying qualities of the character of George Washington.

By knowing the birth date of an individual and seeing if the number of the date is in harmonious vibration with the number given by the name is of considerable help in summing up the general characteristics.

If the number of the birth date and the number given by the name are not in accord, the promise of the man's or woman's career will not be so definite.

Returning to the name of George Washington, as an example, the last digit is the figure 2, with 7 and 4 as the principal digits of the name.

Now, Washington's birthday is celebrated on February 22nd, which makes the double figure in this system to be written as '4-1', with its interchangeable numbers of '2-7' (see Chapter 7). Some people claim that his birth date was February 11th, in the old-style calendar. Should this be the date taken, it would not alter the affect of the number of his name working out to the final digit of a 2, because it was February 22nd, a 4 or February 11th, a 2 both of which are interchangeable numbers with one another, and in consequence the number of the name and the number of the birth *date are in harmonious vibration together.*

If the number of the name and the number of the birth date are not in harmony or accord, it indicates that one is likely to find a jumble or unevenness in the plans and careers of the man or woman whose numbers are not in vibration to one another.

ABRAHAM LINCOLN

Abraham Lincoln was born on February 12th, 1809, an attempt on his life was made on the Friday night of April 14th, 1865, and he died on April 15th.

The name works out as follows :

```
A B R A H A M        L I N C O L N
1 2 2 1 5 1 4        3 1 5 3 7 3 5
-----------------    -----------------
      1 6                   2 7
      ---                   ---
       7              9 = 16 = 7
```

In this case the birth number, the single digit 3, and the single digit of the name are not in harmonious accord.

The single digit of 3 for the birth is a powerful number, being in itself representative of the Planet Jupiter; it indicates underlying ambition, the power to rule and dictate. In describing these persons in Chapter 6, I have stated :

Number 3 people ... are decidedly ambitious; they are never satisfied in being in subordinate positions; their aim is to rise in the world, to have control and authority over others. They are excellent in the execution of commands; they love order and discipline in all things; they readily obey orders themselves, but they also insist on having their orders obeyed. Number 3 people often rise to the very highest positions in any business, profession or sphere in which they may be found. They often excel in positions of authority in the army and navy, in government, and in life generally; and especially in all posts of trust and responsibility, as they are extremely conscientious in carrying out their duties.

The final digit of the name ABRAHAM LINCOLN, a 7, is more weak or gentle in its qualities, as I have stated in Chapter 10 :

People born under the number 7 ... are very independent original, and have strongly marked individuality.. but in everything they do, they sooner or later show a peculiar philosophical outlook on life that tinges all their work.

I further said, number 7 people have 'a peculiar magnetism that has great influence over others.'

The description by this system of Numerology, it must be admitted, accords closely with the well-known character of Abraham Lincoln. Turning to the more mysterious or hidden influences indicated by the compound numbers, if we add the single digit of the birth number, 3, to the digit of the name number, 7, they produce the compound number of 10. In Chapter 14 it is mentioned that ten symbolises the 'Wheel of Fortune.' It is a number of honour, of faith and self-confidence, of rise and fall; one's name will be known for good or evil, according to one's desires, it is a fortunate number in the sense that one's plans are likely to be carried out.

Taking the compound number of the birth, February 12th, for another indication of the occult influences governing this career, it is explained in Chapter 14 that twelve symbolises suffering and anxiety of mind. It is also indicated as 'the Sacrifice' or 'the Victim' and generally foreshadows one being sacrificed for the plans or intrigues of others.

Now, turning to number 16 the compound number of the name, 16, it is mentioned in the same chapter:

The number sixteen has a most peculiar occult symbolism. It is symbolised by a 'Tower Struck by Lightning from which a man is falling with a Crown on his head.' It is also called 'the Shattered Citadel.' It gives warning of some strange fatality awaiting a person.

When one considers Lincoln's sudden assassination as he sat in a box in a theatre on the Friday night of, April 14th, one cannot help being astonished at the truth underlining this system of occult significance of the compound numbers.

Further, Abraham Lincoln was the 16th President of the United States, single digit of this number, the 7, corresponding to the single digit of his name.

FRANKLIN DELANO ROOSEVELT

Franklin Delano Roosevelt, the 32nd President of the United States, was born at Hyde Park, New York, at 8.18 p.m., January 30th, 1882.

The number made by his name are as follows :

```
F R A N K L I N      D E L A N O
8 2 1 5 2 3 1 5      4 5 3 1 5 7
─────────────        ───────────
     2 7                 2 5
     ───                 ───
      9                   7

R  O O S E V E L T
2  7 7 3 5 6 5 3 4
──────────────────
       4 2
       ───
        6  = 22 = 4
```

It will be noticed that his birth date, January 30th, produces for its single digit the powerful number of 3, which my readers will remember stands for the planet Jupiter.

The power of the number 3 is, in his case, afflicted, especially through his early years, by its being in the period of planet Saturn, the 8 negative.

The foundation indicates the following :

Persons born in this part of the Zodiac are generally very active, work for the public good and will often give all they have to relieve the distress of others. They are good reasoners, and are very successful in debate and argument and difficult to convince.

They are excellent in business and finance when they apply their minds to such things, but as a general rule they are more successful for others than for themselves.

They take a great interest in public meetings, large gatherings of people, and public ceremonies.

They have a quiet controlling power with their eyes, and so subdue others. It takes some sudden call of circumstances to make them' make the most of themselves.'

In matter of health they are inclined to suffer from the nerves of the stomach in some peculiar manner that is difficult to relieve by ordinary medicine. They are prone to suffer from accidents to their teeth, pains in the knees and feet and will have trouble *with the middle of the spine*.

Franklin Delano Roosevelt, however, being born under the powerful number of 3, the indicator of strong will, determination, and ambition, was able to rise above the indications given by his Zodiacal Sign, even to conquer the spinal meningitis which attacked him in his early days.

In previous pages of this book describing the qualities of number 3 persons, I have stated :

> Number 3 people, like the number 1 individuals, are decidedly ambitious; they are never satisfied by being in subordinate positions; their aim is to rise in the world, to have control and authority over others. They often rise to the very highest positions in any business, profession or sphere in which they may be found. They often excel in positions of authority in the army and the navy, in government, and in life generally; and especially in all posts of trust and responsibility, as they are extremely conscientious in carrying out their duties.

This appear to be a very fitting description of the 32nd President of the United States.

When we come to analyse the birth and name number, we find, however, they are not in harmony with one another. The birth date, January 30th, is 3, while the name number works out to 22 or the single digit of 4.

President Roosevelt, being the 32nd President was, as the Head of his Nation, under a fortunate compound number—*as far as his country is concerned.* In dealing with the number 32, I have stated in Chapter 14:

> The number has a magical power. It is usually associated with combinations of people or nations. It is a fortunate number if the person it represents holds to his own judgement or opinions; if not, his plans are likely to become wrecked by the stubbornness and stupidity of others. It is a favourable number if it appears in connection with future events.

The compound number of President Roosevelt's name which works out to 22, is, however, not so fortunate *personally*. I have stated in Chapter 14 :

> This number is symbolised by 'good man blinded by the folly of others, with a knapsack on his back full of errors.' It is a warning number of illusion and delusion, a good person who lives in a fool's paradise; a dreamer of dreams who awakens only when surrounded by danger. It is also a number of false judgement owing to the influence of others.

President Roosevelt ran considerable danger of assassination in the course of his career. The indications were very similar to those given in the life of Abraham Lincoln, whose birth number was also 3 in the Zodiacal Sign of Aquarius in the House of Saturn, the negative number 8.

President Roosevelt had a close call from death, when Zangara, the anarchist, fired six shots at him on February 15th, 1933, at Miami, Florida, and Mayor Cermak of Chicago who was by his side got wounded fatally.

NOTE. The title of President is not taken into account in this system of Numerology, as is that of Kings, Queens, hereditary titles or those given for life. The reason being that the title of President is only for a term of years and is therefore a transitory one.

33. THE BIBLE AND NUMBERS

In an earlier chapter of this book, I have given illustrations of the influence of the number 7 and other numbers in connection with the Hebrew race.

One of the great wonders of the world has been the fact that, in spite of privations and persecutions such as no other race ever endured, the Jewish people have held to their religion as set out in the pages of the volume of the *Sacred Law*, and moreover this volume has become *the base of all law in every land and clime into which it has permeated.*

It is acknowledged to have the greatest influence for good of any book that has ever been written. It is considered as the inspired message of God the Creator to the Hebrew race in the first instance, and later to all mankind. In this book, generally called the Bible, more knowledge is at times concealed than is revealed to the ordinary reader.

For me, it will be sufficient in the short space at my disposal if I am able to call attention to one single instance, but one of radiant importance, to prove that this wonderful book not only has in its pages the evidence of Divine Design in the Creator's construction of things but that *it contains in itself a systematic plan and design* that must carry with it incontrovertible proof that not only is the Bible inspired, but that it has within *itself the proofs of its inspiration,* so that all mankind might believe in its message.

It has been handed down to us that the first books of the Bible were written or compiled by one of the greatest men of all time, a man called Moses. Let us consider for a moment who this man was and what his claims are for universal respect and admiration. He was born of the priestly house of Levi. He was called Moses because Pharaoh's daughter saved him from the waters of the Nile. He was adopted by *her and became her son.*

In this position, as the child of the great Pharoah's daughter, he received the highest education that was possible in that wonderful land of Egypt. The Bible tells us 'he was versed in all the wisdom of the Egyptians.' History tells us that he became a Master of Astrology, that he erected a great observatory in the Temple of the Sun at Heliopolis.

When his supposed mother became the Queen of Egypt, Moses became the commander-in-chief of her army; as such he conquered the Ethiopians and relieved Egypt from the danger of invasion.

In this moment of triumph the Queen died, a Pharaoh came to the throne who 'knew not Moses,' and the Bible says, 'he went out unto his brethren and looked on their burdens.' The 'call of the blood' had come; he knew he was a Hebrew, the son of the priestly tribe of Levi; 'he saw an Egyptian smiting one of his brethren;'[1] he slew the Egyptian and took refuge in the land of Midian.

Moses was now eighty years of age[2], a man of experience, a man accustomed to the responsibility and power, a man of great learning, 'versed in all the wisdom of the Egyptians.' Such was the man the Lord had chosen for the delivery of His people.

I will pass over the message from 'the burning bush,' that command that has passed down through the ages : 'I AM that I AM.'

I must leave to the imagination of my readers the humbling of Pharaoh by the ten plagues, the passover night, the outward march of that multitude of men, women, and herds of cattle. No one but Moses, who had been a commander-in-chief, could have organised such a march.

What a milestone in history—the first passover of the Hebrews as a nation. What a meaning it must have had for a people in slavery.

The end of four hundred and thirty years of bondage to the Egyptians, 'that night of the Lord to be observed of all the children of Israel in their generation.'[3]

The first great passover of the Hebrews took place at the full moon after the Spring Equinox in the first month of the Hebraic year, the month which is called Abib. If one looks at an atlas containing the old Hebrew names, it is easy to see that Moses skilfully led this great multitude of people towards the most formidable part of the Red Sea at northern end of the Gulf of Suez, at a place called Pi-hahiroth, as stated in the Bible.[4]

---

[1] Exodus ii. 11.
[2] Ibid, vii. 7.
[3] Ibid, xii. 42.
[4] Ibid, xiv. 2.

Moses was well acquainted with this part of the country, having passed this way on his flight to Midian and his return to Egypt. He had observed the influx of the tides, and by his astrological calculations he knew that the south-eastern monsoon would arrive at a certain date to aid his plans. This is the east wind mentioned in the English version of the Bible; in the Septuagint, it is called a strong southern wind; but both in poetical description is the same, 'and the Lord caused the sea to go back by a strong east wind all that night and made the sea dry land and the waters were divided[1] and the children of Israel walked upon dry land in the midst of the sea.'

After this came that mysterious forty years of wandering in the desert which was planned and designed to purge the Israelites from the false teachings they had imbibed during their four hundred years of residence among the religions of Egypt.

If one again looks at any Old Testament map, one cannot help but remark how short the distance would have been had Moses led his people *directly across to Palestine.* Instead they were made to traverse the whole peninsula of Sinai before they were allowed to turn their faces towards the 'Promised Land.'

During that forty years of wandering a generation had passed away. Wisely and designedly the older race who had been contaminated by their long sojourn in Egypt had been 'gathered to their fathers.' Their place had been taken by the fresh blood of their sons and daughters, a younger generation more fitted to understand the teachings of the Great Law Giver—more fitted as 'a chosen race,' later on to hand down to posterity the pages of a sacred volume which was destined to illuminate and influence all races of mankind as well as their own.

It is my privilege to draw attention to this law of mysterious and wonderful design. It is more exemplified in the happenings and history of the Hebrew people than any other. If this race had been created for no other purpose than this, their sufferings and privations have not been in vain.

In those far-off ages when Moses collected and put together the records of God's dealings with the children of Israel, the volumes of the Sacred Law was not divided into chapters and verses. Later still, David, the man who was specially chosen by God to be King of the Israelites,

---

[1] Exodus xiv. 21.

in writing the Psalms, could not by any natural means have surmised that when the Bible, some two thousands years after his death, came to be divided into chapters, the 119th Psalm would become *the longest chapter of the entire Book*, especially as scarcely one half of the Sacred Volume existed in his time.

This Psalm consists of 176 verses, every one of which directly or indirectly calls attention to the precepts laid down in the entire book.

The Psalm itself is, by some mysterious law of calculation, divided into 22 sections, the exact number of the letters that compose the Hebrew alphabet. Each section is subdivided into 8 verses, each verse being an iambic tetrameter, namely 16 syllables alternately short and long[1].

Still more extraordinary is the first fact that every one of the 8 verses of the first section begins with the first letter of the Hebrew alphabet : Aleph.

The 8 verses of the second section begin with the second letter of the Hebrew alphabet : Beth.

The 8 verses of the third section begin with the third letter of the alphabet : Gimel.

This extraordinary precision continues until all the 22 letters of the Hebrew alphabet are employed.

When this wonderful chapter thousands of years later came to be translated into other languages, it was found that no other language could fit in with this rule. Therefore the Hebrew letters were set out simply as titles at the head of each of the eight sections, as may be seen if anyone looks up the 119th Psalm.

In the millions and millions of books that have been printed, there is *not one example in the world* of such an acrostic having ever been made or of such an attempt having been thought of to call attention to the longest chapter calls direct notice in one form of another to the good to be derived from following the precepts laid down in the volume of the *Sacred Law*. Further, every verse alludes in some part of it to the Divine influence underlying the whole.

Example : The first verse contains the words 'the law of the Lord.'
The 2nd verse, 'His testimonies.'
The 3rd verse, 'His ways.'

---

[1] I am speaking of course, of the Hebrew original version

The 4th verse, 'Thy precepts'
The 5th verse, 'Thy statutes'
The 6th verse, 'Thy Commandments.'
The 7th verse, 'Thy righteous judgements.'
The 8nd verse, 'Thy statutes.'
This continues through the entire 22 sections.

The mystic number of 12 appears in the root words employed, which are Statutes ordinances, Faithfulness, Surety, Law, Name, Word, Precepts, Ways, Judgements, Testimonies, Commandements, and at least *one of these* 12 *words* are unerringly found in each of the 176 verses.

In the English version of the two longest words employed are representative of the Bible, namely 'Thy commandments' and 'Thy testimonies.' In their uses in this Psalm they present a strange coincidence with the 22 sections of the Psalm and the 22 letters of the original Hebrew alphabet. The word 'commandments' is employed either in the singular or in the plural exactly *22 times*, while 'testimonies' is used *22 times in the plural* and once in the singular at the end of the first half of the Psalm, namely the end of the 88th verse, which number *is itself a multiple of 22.*

Now, let me sum up my observations on this, the most extraordinary example of *design* in literature written or printed that has even been known. One cannot believe that such a thing could happen by chance; equally one cannot believe that some mortal, no matter how gifted, could have created a psalm in the form of an acrostic unmatched in the literature of the world, past or present; still more so, that this psalm *should be designed* to be the longest chapter in a book *not then completed.*

And yet I have not exhausted all the features that call attention to this example of design.

It may not have been noticed before, by the many people who have read the Bible through from cover to cover, that both *the shortest* and *the longest chapters* of this wonderful book are placed in *close proximity to each other,* the shortest being the 117th and the longest the 119th Psalm. Now the one intermediary chapter between the shortest and the longest, the 118th, presents in itself such a number of remarkable coincidences that one is forced to the conclusion that these three psalms *were purposely planned to come together for a definite reason—that* reason evidently being that the relation of such coincidences would sooner or later strike some searcher of truth, as an illustration of Divine

Design and consequently prove of the Divine Inspiration that guided not only the writer of the Psalms, but thousands of years later *the translators of this books into other languages.*

The 118th Psalm, occupying as it does the remarkable position of being between the shortest and longest chapters of the Bible, actually contains *the middle or central verse of the entire Bible.* This, the middle verse of the Sacred Book, is the 8th verse of the 118th Psalm.[1]

Its words are significant in their meaning—they are an epitome of the great truth taught all through the preceding chapters or those that follow: 'It is better to trust in the Lord than to put confidence in man.'

Further, if one writes down in figures Psalm 118, verse 8, and puts these numbers side by side, they become 1188, which is the *exact number of chapters in the Bible,* besides the one that contains the remarkable verse above quoted and which, as I mentioned before, *is the middle verse of the entire book.*

Next to this 118th Psalm, the 117th stands out as the shortest chapter of the Bible, and not only is this a curious fact, but it is still doubly so, by being at the same time *the central chapter* of the Book, having exactly as many chapters before it as after it.

The most accurate way of finding out if the 117th Psalm is the central chapter of the Bible is to refer to the table usually printed in the beginning of the Authorised Version. This table contains six columns or 39 books of the Old Testament and 27 books of the New. By adding together the numbers of chapters given by those six columns we get the number 1189, the total number of the chapters in the Bible, the middle one must therefore be the 595th, as there cannot be anything else than 594 chapters before it and 594 following it.

The very number 595, which is the number of the 117th Psalm, calculated as a chapter of the Bible, conveys in itself the idea of perfect symmetry, namely it can be read the same way whether from left to right or vice versa; it represents in itself *the principle of perfect equilibrium* which consists of equal disposition of the parts of both sides of the centre.

---

[1]The actual form and division of the Bible is the work of different minds, widely separated by time, by countries, by training. There can therefore be not question of collusion in the carrying out of the evident design that underlies the construction of the Bible.

This, the shortest chapter in the Bible and the central one of the entire Book, has a striking significance of its own :

O praise the Lord all ye nations; praise Him all ye people. For His merciful kindness is great towards us ; and the truth of the Lord endureth for ever.

One should not regard the extraordinary examples I have set out in these pages as isolated cases of mere coincidence, for when taken together, as they were evidently intended to be, they give the key to the construction of the Bible itself as a marvellous example of Divine inspiration. They tend to show that these three Psalms must have been written with a plan of forming these coincidences for some given purpose, and that the division and numeration of the entire Bible, so perfect in every way, *was prearranged* before even the greater part of it had been written by those who lived in later ages.

34. CONCLUSION

It naturally follows that if a person makes a special study of any one subject, from long experience, cultivation and studious research, he will in the end unravel, at least to some extent, the so-called mysteries of the subject on which he has so concentrated his attention.

To the student of Art, it reveals her mysteries of colour, form, design, pose, and a thousand and one subtleties that escape the ordinary observer. To the student of Biology every leaf tells its own story, every tree its age, every flower its own pedigree.

To the student of Science, what is magic to the uninitated becomes a natural phenomenon with general laws, governed by rules or calculations that all who choose can learn and understand.

In presenting this book to the public I need then offer no other reason than of having been a student of this particular branch of thought for a very long period, and having proved the so-called theories by countless experiments and experiences, I feel I am at last in a position to give to the world at large the result of such studies.

It is generally admitted that the occult side of things has been the one side of life that has been the least explored or investigated. That there is an occult or hidden part in actual relation to human life is a fact conceded to, but before this mystery—the greatest of all—the majority of thinkers have held themselves aloof.

In our age the physical and mechanical sciences have called for the greatest attention, yet such things as wireless communication and radium, which have become the household word today, have been stumbled across by the so-called chance.

Already wireless communication has saved hundreds of lives, radium has done likewise, the mysteries of yesterday have become the commonplace of today, and so knowledge in the eternal fitness of things becomes the servant of those who serve.

In pursuit of the laws which have controlled the thought in recent centuries, man has, in earning his successes on the physical and mechanical plane, forgotten the loss he has sustained from the lack of study and observation of the occult or psychic side of humanity. He is more occupied today in building implements for the destruction of life than he is in the problems of life itself or in the finding out of those laws which create, control, and sustain life.

When Newton discovered gravitation, it was not supposed for a moment that he had solved the problem of the spheres, and it is sometimes forgotten that when he came to realise that beyond our system of stars, sun, moon and planets there were again the 'fixed stars' with their countless systems. Amidst the magnitude of the problem, he could only decide that there was again some occult law behind all, greater than any known law that could ever be imagined.

I trust my readers who have followed my theories through this book, have grasped the fundamental fact underlying these pages, that the knowledge I have endeavoured to give to the public is of *a practical nature* with the decided object of helping my fellow men to make the best of themselves and lead their lives as successfully as possible.

Uptill now occultism has been associated with the idea that its students must belong to the domain of dreamers of dreams or those who live in some world of their own. In consequence of this idea the average 'man in the street' has put aside such studies as not useful, impractical or belonging to the money-making side of life.

It has also been drummed into his ears that all such studies bordered on witchcraft and were in some way or the other associated with the Devil.

Being brought up to go to church every Sunday and hearing every time he went that he was 'a miserable sinner,' doomed to punishment and torment both in this life and that to come, he in the end believed that he was 'a miserable sinner,' and so dared not seek for any knowledge that might enable him to shake off the chains of conventionality and customs that grounded him down and kept him in mental and intellectual slavery.

He had perhaps no means to know that some of the greatest kings of the world owed their success and wealth to advice given by their Astrologers or that the Egyptian Magicians had greater power than *either priest or potentate. He had perhaps never read that the great* Queen Elizabeth consulted her astrologer and palmist, Dr. John Dee, on all important matters of States, and that the destiny of England had been guided from time to time by those students of occultism whom he had been taught to believe were but fit companions for black cats, and were workers of the Devil.

He had perhaps never read of that great English astrologer, William Lilly, who had predicted the Fire of London, *fifteen years before it took place* or that the House of Commons had called him before that great assembly believing that as he had predicted the calamity with such accuracy, he could explain to them what had caused such a catastrophe.

Further, his English History had never told him that Charles I had given the first thousand pounds his government sent him to Hampton Court to the same Lilly, the astrologer, asking him to predict his fate, and that had the king taken the warnings given to him by Astrology he would not have lost his head and descended to posterity as 'Charles the Martyr.'

In all probability he never knew that Queen Anne maintained an astrologer upon the roll of the Privy Purse, and that she had such faith in the celebrated Von Galgebrok that she asked him to predict the year of her death. This he did with perfect accuracy three years before the event, which took place on 1st August, 1714.

Life is but the child of Mystery—we know not its origin—we know not its end. We see 'as in a darkly glass' the threads of Destiny weaving the known and the unknown —and we wonder why.

We feel there is Design in all things—but it is only in looking back on the past that the wonders of 'the pattern' become manifest.

We are indeed 'of little faith,' we children of men. We forget that we were made 'in the image and likeness of God,' and, in forgetting that, we have sold our birthright for 'the mess of pottage' of man-made beliefs. We do not dare to think of ourselves, for our 'teachers' alone have wisdom ? But alas! they locked the doors of knowledge, and the keys have rusted for want of use.

Behind all—the Gods of Patience—the God of Eternity—waits.

Slowly the ages pass: 'A thousand years are but a day.' Nations rise and fall. Teachers come and go. Time weaves Destiny into Design until in the end Perfection shines through the wrap and weft and the *God thought underlying all becomes manifest.*

If, then one of the so-called 'occult studies,' such as I have tried to explain, has helped to call attention to those hidden laws of life that illustrate the Divine Design, then when 'the Call' comes—I will go my way, content that the years of study I have given to this work were not wasted and were not in vain.

I have seen so many wrecked and broken lives, where, had the people possessed even a slight knowledge of their own dispositions, they might have been saved, that I have felt it a duty to publish in a cheap and simple form the indications of character and tendencies which may be easily learned by a study of these 'periods of birth.'

I believe that any aid that may help towards the observation of character is *not only useful but even essential if one wishes to keep abreast and succeed in this age of ever-increasing competition.*

Those people who have some means at their command to learn their own characters and the dispositions of others must certainly be thrice armed in the battle of life, and consequently more successful than the people who know nothing of such things. Therefore I have no hesitation in saying that with this book in one's possession, one has a means towards winning success and also happiness.

With even a slight knowledge of what I designate in these pages as Life's Natural Affinities, the road to the divorce courts would not be so crowded as it is at present, parents would more easily understand their children and children their parents, and a great deal of suffering and friction might be avoided.

In conclusion, I trust I am not presuming too much when I venture to hope that this unpretentious volume may be the means of helping a large proportion of my fellow-beings to realise that in the study of the mysteries of life we are giving praise and glory to the Creator of Life, who in His infinite wisdom created all things to be used by man for the highest development of his kind.

PERSONALITY DEVELOPMENT

4th Idiot
Author: B. R. Chowdhary
Rs. 150

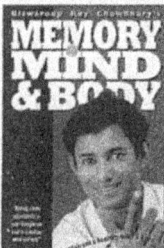
Memory Mind & Body
Author: B. R. Chowdhary
Rs. 195

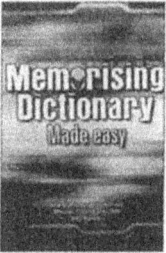
Memorising Dictionary Made Easy
Author: B. R. Chowdhary
Rs. 150

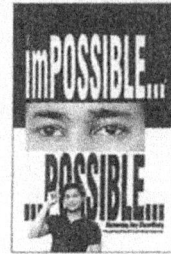
Impossible... Possible...
Author: B. R. Chowdhary
Rs. 150

Memory Unlimited
Author: B. R. Chowdhary
Rs. 150

Dynamic Memory Methods
Author: B. R. Chowdhary
Rs. 150

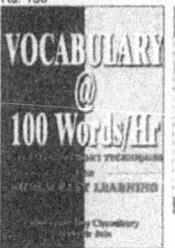
Vocabulary @ 100 words/Hr.
Author: B. R. Chowdhary
Rs. 95

One Minute Memory Mind Manager
Author: B. R. Chowdhary
Rs. 75

Turn Your Creative Spark Into a Flame
Author: Joginder Singh
Rs. 95

How To Excel When Chips Are Down
Author: Joginder Singh
Rs. 95

Winning Ways
Author: Joginder Singh
Rs. 150

Success Mantra
Author: Joginder Singh
Rs. 150

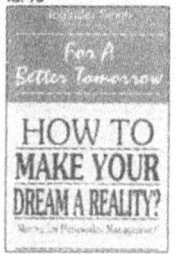
For A Better Tomorrow
Author: Joginder Singh
Rs. 150

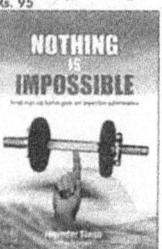
Nothing is Impossible
Author: Joginder Singh
Rs. 150

Think Big Become Big
Author: Tarun Engineer
Rs. 150

Memory Techniques For science students
Author: N. Roy Chowdhury
Rs. 95

 DIAMOND BOOKS X-30, Okhla Industrial Area, Phase-II, New Delhi-110020, Phones: 41611861- 65, 40712100, Fax: 011- 41611866
E-mail: Sales@dpb.in, Website: www.dpb.in

DIAMOND POCKET BOOKS PRESENTS

A Guide to Tax Planning
R.N. Lakhotia, Subhash Lakhotia

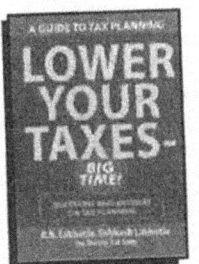

The book contains answers on hundreds of points relating to different facets of Income-tax Planning. In the book, a large number of tax paying public of India sitting at home, will be able to enjoy all the solutions to their intricate problems in connection with Income-tax Planning.

Price : 150.00

Spiritualism in Day-to-Day Life

This extremely comprehensive self-help book is user-friendly, and gets right to the point in presenting coping techniques for practically every life problem. This how-to book provides therapy to counter the tension people feel when depressed and lonely. And most important of all, it shows us how spiritualism can change the way we react to stress, and how this helps decrease chances of suffering.

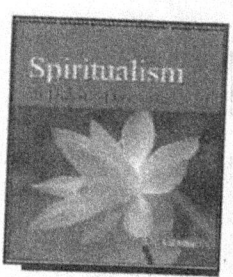

50.00

Vegetarianism in Day-to-Day Life

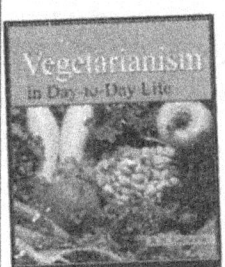

More and more people all over the world are turning vegetarian in order to be fit for life. There is growing acceptance that vegetarianism is a more modern, scientific and better way of living than "flesh eating". This book gives you up-to-date information on the benefits of vegetarianism -how, apart from being more economical, it reduces the chances of cancer, heart attacks and other deadly diseases.

50.00

Diamond Pocket Books (P) Ltd.
X-30, Okhla Industrial Area, Phase-II, New Delhi-110020,
Phones : 011-41611861, 40712100, Fax :011- 41611866
E-mail : Sales@dpb.in, Website: www.dpb.in

Excellent Books On Personality Development

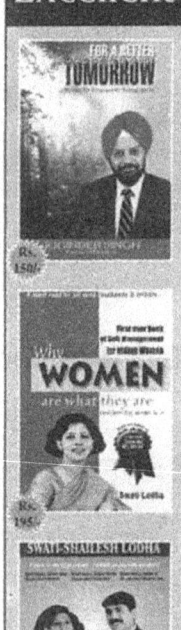

FOR A BETTER TOMORROW
By: Joginder Singh (Former CBI Director)

This magnum opus by Sh. Joginder Singh is a treatise on self improvement. This win-win sotry is based on the secrets of success as to how to become an achiever. And the success mantra that he espouses for you: Make the best of all opportunities; dream big and work hard—dreams will turn sheer realities. You only need to hone your skills and attitude to become a winner.

Price: Rs. 150/-

WHY WOMEN ARE WHAT THEY ARE
By: Swati Lodha

A book which empowers women to command a unique status, dignity and respect for herself. If you are a daughter, wife or a mother this book will hold your hand and guide you. If you are a son, husband or a father, this book will motivate towards perfection in these roles.

Price: Rs. 195/-

COME ON! GET SET GO...
By: Swati-Shailesh Lodha

This book reveals your real self. It tells you about the hairline difference between a person who is a real success and the one who pretends to be so. This book prompts you to discover yourself. This book doesn't make you "The Best" but it makes you "Second to None".

Price: Rs. 195/-

THE EXCELLENCE IN YOU
By: Dr. Giriraj Shah

This book teaches you to do the same manage your life as a whole. It tells you about your aims in life, how sincerity and perseverance help you to achieve those aims. It teaches you how your presence of mind can make you perfect. It also tells you about various etiquettes, and mannerisms to be used in life.

Price: Rs. 150/-

THE SECRET OF HAPPINESS
By: Jas Mand

This book does not endorse any religious methodology to achieved a state of bliss as most religions claim. The author has attempted to approach the subject of happiness from the scientific angle of a rationalist. Unlike self-help books, it does not offer first-aid. It proposes regular and non-stop work on your growth all the time. The basic emphasis is on cultivating the attitude of happiness, which primarily is in one's own hands.

Price: Rs. 195/-

Ⓒ Fusion Books
X-30, Okhla Industrial Area, Phase-II, New Delhi-110020, Ph.: 41611861, Fax: 41611861,
E-mail: sales@diamondpublication.com, Website: www.diamondpublication.com

BEST BOOKS ON PERSONALITY DEVELOPMENT

MANAGEMENT GURU BHAGWAN SRI RAM
Dr. Sunil Jogi

Management Guru Bhagwan Sri Ram is a marvellous book written by the acclaimed author Dr. Sunil Jogi. In this book, a number of management tips of Bhagwan Ram have been discussed in details. Management Guru Ram achieved unique management skills through self-restraint and politeness. He is a theist. So, this book will certainly be a source of inspiration to the new generation.

Price : 95.00

A GUIDE TO NETWORK MARKETING
Surya Sinha

This book will prove to be a milestone to all those who are already associated with or desire to join this Business. It has been written in a simple language and manner by the well known thinker, inspirer & human trainer Surya Sinha.

Price : 100.00

WHY NETWORK MARKETING
Surya Sinha

In this book, you will know how network marketing works. How to earn extra income, economic freedom, self employment, time freedom, personality Development, helping others, making new contacts learning Inheritance..

Price : 150.00

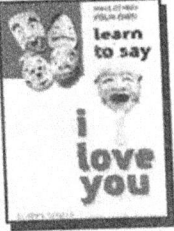

LEARN TO SAY I LOVE YOU
Surya Sinha

The book is meant to make you more practical, professional and well-connected. The book - Learn to say I Love You- bridges distance, eliminates isolation and inculcates in us a new feelings and a new thinking, for our all round happiness and success.

Rs. 150.00

HAVE GUTS
Jaswin Jassi

This is a true story, about the author's tryst with life. From birth till his present day situation, it talks about how at a tender age of 10, he became a man and shouldered responsibilities of the family. How he grew up to face the storm in the eye and paved his own path.

Rs. 95.00

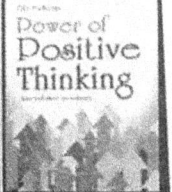

POWER OF POSITIVE THINKING
G.D. Budhiraja

Leading a split life has been one of the greatest problems down the ages and that is why the humanity seems sick today. When there is chasm between awareness and expression in our behaviour, we become unauthentic. **Rs. 95.00**

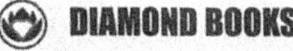 **DIAMOND BOOKS** X-30, Okhla Industrial Area, Phase-II, New Delhi-110020, Phones : 41611861- 65, 40712100, Fax: 011- 41611866
E-mail : Sales@dpb.in, Website: www.dpb.in

Now you can
Improve your Memory

Without problem
choose book of your favourite author
Biswaroop Roy Chowdhury

One Minute Mind Memory
In the present spell of highly competitive time, where knowledge, qualifications and skills are so richly available is people, the next parameter which can decide the overall merit is memory. It is an art of quick retrival of what you have in the stock of your mind. Means what you have is alright, but what you can pull out instantly from your mind system, on the hour of need, is paid most. This book is designed to make your mind capable to earn that premium.

Invisible Doctor
This book tells about the doctors, medical researchers, and the hundreds of other people who have used me to cure a huge variety of illnesses and combat even the most incurable diseases. The authors of the book Biswaroop Roy Chowdhury and B K Chandra Shekhar.

Memory Unlimited
This book is a collection of examples from various areas of science, commerce and arts showing how Advanced Mnemonics can be helpful in improving the learning speed.

Memory, Mind & Body
Memory, Mind & Body is the masterpiece by a master mind. It is another magnum opus by the renowed memory master. Biswaroop Roy Chowdhury, whose amazing work Dynamic Memory Methods was a record-breaking bestseller of the millennium, running into several reprints in a short span.

Dynamic Memory Methods
Dynamic Memory Methods is a bestseller on memory developing techniques. This book deals with the use of scientific memory techniques. This book deals with the use of scientific memory techniques for memorising faster and retaining it longer.

Impossible.. Possible...
This book is about change. Poeple by nature are status quoists. This book will tell you how you can change the way you think, act and behave. The chronic patients can recover, the habitual failures can turn around.

Vocabulary@100 Words/hr
Whether you are a businessman, or a student, if you want to remember everything this book is a must for you. It deals with how to improve concentration Memorising difficult biological diagrams.

Memorising Dictionary Made Easy
Memorising Dictionary Made Easy will be immensely useful to all. The book identifies every new word with a Key and Memory Link, which connect the new word with a more identifiable word and in the process get firmly lodged in the reader's mind.

Books can be requisitioned by V.P.P. Postage charges will be Rs. 20/- per book.
For orders of three books the postage will be free.

FUSION BOOKS X-30, Okhla Industrial Area, Phase-II, New Delhi-110020.
Phone : 41611861 Fax : 41611866
E-mail : sales@dpb.in Website : www.dpb.in

www.ingramcontent.com/pod-product-compliance
Lightning Source LLC
LaVergne TN
LVHW091303080426
835510LV00007B/369